I0790510

FROM DESCENDANTS OF SLAVES TO MASS INCARCERATION

TABITHA ELLIS

WESTBOW PRESS
A DIVISION OF THOMAS NELSON
& ZONDERVAN

WestBow Press books may be ordered through booksellers or by contacting:

WestBow Press
A Division of Thomas Nelson & Zondervan
1663 Liberty Drive
Bloomington, IN 47403
www.westbowpress.com
844-714-3454

All Scriptures are taken from King James version of the Bible, public domain.

ISBN: 978-1-6642-9717-3 (sc)
ISBN: 978-1-6642-9718-0 (e)
ISBN: 979-8-3850-1116-2 (hc)

Library of Congress Control Number: 2023920860

Print information available on the last page.

WestBow Press rev. date: 3/5/2024

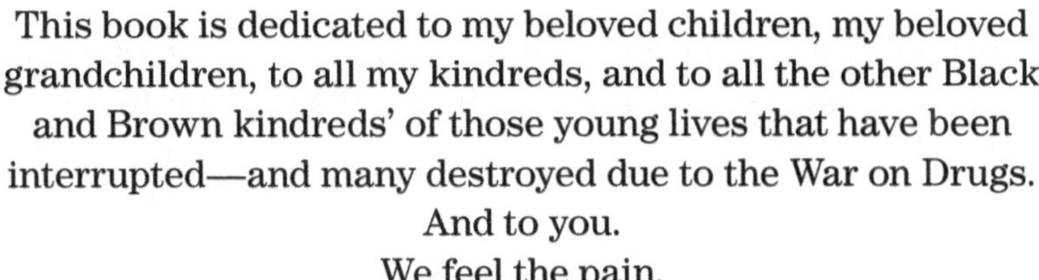

This book is dedicated to my beloved children, my beloved grandchildren, to all my kindreds, and to all the other Black and Brown kindreds' of those young lives that have been interrupted—and many destroyed due to the War on Drugs.
And to you.
We feel the pain.

"For how can I endure to see the evil that shall come unto my people? Or how can I endure to see the destruction of my kindred?"

Esther 8:6 (KJV)

CONTENTS

A NOTE TO THE READER

Michelle Alexander, one of the authors I've quoted, has three books I used as sources.

All three books have the same title *The New Jim Crow: Mass Incarceration in the Age of Colorblindness*. All three have different publications dates.

To go straight to the specific book and page where I found the quote, check the two publisher dates on the back side of the Title page as printed here.

(Alexander 2010, 2011, page)
(Alexander 2010, 2012, page)
(Alexander 2020, page)

PREFACE

I'm sure there are many, many, many Blacks like me who had never imagined a loved one or a friend being entrapped in the criminal justice system. This is my personal belief regarding The War on Drugs. The drug war is just a continuation of premeditated intentions to put droves of young Blacks behind bars. That's what has happened. My belief is from several happenings in my past. It's from life-long experiences as a Black female; from stories I heard from my parents and other older relatives; from studying Black history; and from observing the legislation of many laws and policies that have resulted in the capture of Black and Brown men as "the favorite whipping boys.'

From all that mentioned above, I agree with Michelle Alexander's report that, "Since the days of slavery, Black men have been depicted and understood as criminals", Michelle Alexander, *The New Jim Crow: Mass Incarceration in the Age of Colorblindness* (The New Press, 2020) 208. That "criminal nature," in the minds of former slave holders and some of their offspring, has continued throughout centuries in many minds to justify their criminal treatment. The criminal justice system is just the institution now designed to continue that trend from slavery. That so-called "criminal nature", in my opinion, is still in the minds of some former slaveholders and some of their offspring. To repeat, that attitude has continued throughout centuries in many minds.

My analysis is that running away from the "massa" was a crime, back when police were appointed to catch runaway slaves early in the Republic. It was a crime to cause white men economic loss. Slaves were their property. Running away affected the master's bottom line.

In the War on Drugs, that "criminal nature" is still the trend of thinking for many who want to put young Black descendants of slaves behind bars now. Police target young Blacks for drug crimes now, since there are no more runaway slaves. Many still assume that the young Black man is just bad, a natural villain in whatever context, but that's not so. It maybe the subconscious bothering some because of how the Black man has been treated in the past.

In my view, not much has changed. Millions of dollars are being legislated for the War on Drugs, just like slavery was well-funded by the government. Making a profit off the misery of others is still a high priority, whether the administration in power is Republican or Democratic. Blacks have always been the overwhelming inmates represented. According to Michelle Alexander, (2010, 2012, 180), "More black men are imprisoned today than at any other moment in our nation's history". Why? Where's the progress? Either somebody can't count or has a strange way of measuring progress. Going to a court hearing for the first time at age seventy-nine to support a loved one, Sherman, who was arrested, convicted, and locked behind bars; then visiting with him once as an inmate, stirred me passionately to write about what I saw and heard with my own eyes and ears in the criminal justice system. It's quite different when this happens to someone you love and it's not to someone else you're watching on the news. My research uncovered what I saw to be blatant, biased, unequal enforcement of justice under the laws and policies legislated and funded by the United States government. It is not much like the only criminal justice TV show, *Perry Mason*, I ever watched in the late 1950s. I can't remember seeing all those cells mostly full of Black young men.

My views in this project are through my own lens, those of a just-turned-eighty-year-old high-functioning African-American who loves all her family, and Black people in general. I am beyond angry at the government's entrapment process that has captured so many of our young Black men with all these racist laws, then taking my tax dollars to pay for keeping my loved one behind bars due to the very unjust, evil, racist War on Drugs for which he was arrested. I believe the program was advanced because research notes that crime was declining. There weren't as many murders and other crimes bringing in much money. Murder charges brought in no federal dollars, but drug charges did. Sherman's imprisonment was said to keep the streets safe, though the crime was categorized as non-violent. To me, a violent person could be a villain. If the act is non-violent and there's no physical injury, why all the heavy tanks and guns to protect someone from non-violent behavior?

I believe in the Bible. That's my compass—where I get my directions for living and "the courage to be." It is my motivation. Others might get theirs from their whims, imagination, or from whatever they feel or have heard. I know that when God made humans in his own image, that included Black folks, too. God said what he made was good. I do not believe I came from sludge or evolved from apes with the mind I have. I don't believe an ape thinks like a human being. Surely, God, with his omniscience (knowing all things) knows if he wants to make a horse or a man or a chicken or an ape.

Yet, so many (but not all white folks outside or within the reigns of power) seem to have the same imagination to discriminate against Blacks. It seems like there's a master mindset plan to hinder, stop, or make it hard for Blacks to do much of whatever they desire in any area. To the contrary, I am unaware of another race trying to hinder or place hurdles in the path of white folk because of the color of their skin, and telling them what they can't do. They don't have to think about being chased by biased law officers and shot sixty times in the name of law and order. I've never heard of a white male being shot sixty times before he's captured.

I heard on the news that the United States has only 5 percent of the world's population but 25 percent of the world's prisoners, most of whom are Black. You can visit most any U.S. prison and see for yourself who's locked up.

According to Alexander, "nothing has contributed more to the systematic mass incarceration of people of color [especially Black] in the U.S. than the War on Drugs" (Alexander 2020, 60). My view is that crimes were created explicitly for that massive program, so law enforcement could capture young (especially Black) men and take them away with guns and handcuffs, undermining their right under the Declaration of Independence for the pursuit of happiness just because they can. This is done so this country can continue to profit off the misery of people of color, especially Blacks. The only reason is that a lot of white leaders have that outrageous greed for money and power. That desire to legislate against and punish primarily Blacks just because you can, is ill-natured and cruel, akin to Hitler, just as in colonial times.

This country was built by putting people from Africa in chains in slavery, mostly without paying them for their labor. Now this system is still being maintained in large part, overwhelming by young Black men subsisting on next to nothing because handcuffs backed up with guns forced them into captivity under the cover of the War on Drugs. In my opinion, this is just as unjust and racist as slavery, when chains were used to take away slaves' freedom.

It seems that our legislators feel that young Black men, among all the young folk in the U.S., are most in need of houses of correction. They are the ones arrested and convicted of drug offenses at rates far out of proportion to their crimes. They make up 14 percent of the total U.S. population, yet did you know that "almost half of all prisoners in the U.S. at any given time are Black?" Manning Marable, *How Capitalism Underdeveloped*

Black America (Haymarket Books, 1983) 112. This is only 14 percent of the population, as mentioned above.

When I was in high school in the late 1950s, I didn't know a classmate in jail. Therefore, I can attest that in the years since then in the criminal justice system, racism has gotten worse. There are still so many whites who have that greed, self-interest, and outrageous resentment towards Blacks, akin to Hitler's hatred toward the Jews. Anyone can visit the jails and prisons and see for themselves who is behind bars.

"One in three young African-American men will serve time in prison if current trends continue", states (Alexander, 2010, 2012, 9). Other research notes that one in three young Black men is currently under the control of the criminal justice system, in jail, in prison, on probation, or parole. Ms. Alexander continues that "more Black men are imprisoned today [the 2000s] than at any moment in our nation's history" (180). She also states that "Officers were under tremendous pressure from their commander to keep their arrest numbers up" (80).

In Black communities similar to Washington D.C. and all across America, "it is estimated that 3 of 4 young Black men (and nearly all those in the poorest neighborhoods) can expect to serve time in prison" (Alexander, 2010, 2011, 6).

Alexander contends also that Blacks are not offending anymore. Disparities in law enforcement have caused this mass incarceration. Many young men of color (especially Black) have been put behind bars, due to the continued "biased law enforcement practices" (Alexander, 2010, 2012, 187).

"Racially biased police discretion…is how…the majority of people who get swept into the criminal justice system in the War on Drugs turn out to be Black or Brown—even though police adamantly deny that they engage in racial profiling", (Alexander, 2010, 2012, 123). Why else would mass drug arrests be concentrated in the impoverished urban areas? Federal dollars continue to go to those departments where police go looking in the hood for drugs and to capture young Blacks.

There's a pandemic of racism that was brought to colonial America from Europe. There may be other published works on this subject that differ. However, Ibram X. Kendi "narrates the entire history of racist ideas from their origins in fifteenth-century Europe, through colonial times when the early British settlers carried racist ideas to America," Ibram X. Kendi, *Stamped from the Beginning* (Nation Books, 2016) 6.

Kendi, an assistant professor of African American History and award-winning historian, reports that racist ideas were created to rationalize the nation's racial inequalities. He states further that "during America's first century, racist theological ideas…sanctioned the growth of American slavery and made it acceptable to the Christian churches", (Kendi, 6). History notes that Cotton Mather (1663–1728), a Puritan, preached "racial inequality in body while insisting that the dark souls of enslaved Africans would become white when they became Christians" (Kendi, 6). His writings and those of Richard Mather "helped carry two-hundred-year-old racist ideas from Europe across the Atlantic Ocean." The report also states that Cotton Mather's "writings and sermons were widely read in the colonies and in Europe" (Kendi, 6). Politicians in the U.S. justified slavery.

Returning to Sherman, navigating through this pandemic can be a daunting task for many Afro-American youth. I personally witnessed this being involved with Sherman, one of my many Black male loved ones. My pastor gave me permission to use that terminology "pandemic of racism," which he used in his sermon one Sunday morning.

The pandemic of racism has affected many in varying degrees for centuries, resulting in a great loss of Black life. However, there's no government entity or study that I've researched or heard about being formed to try to find a cure like has been done for the COVID-19 pandemic.

Studies of all kinds of human behavior (normal and abnormal) have invested in a variety of problems. Out of all the great minds in this nation and its allies, no one I've learned about in research has found a cure for or helped control the damage from the pandemic of racism, especially on Blacks.

There have been many great inventions. Thomas Edison invented the electric light that changed the lives of millions of people. Albert Einstein, who was born in Germany, became an American citizen in 1940. He did work that led to the atomic bomb in 1945. Then there was Jonas E. Salk, an American research scientist, who did work in the field of preventative medicine. He gained his greatest recognition for developing a vaccine against polio.

From reading those and the discoveries of others, there's no shortage of great minds and brilliant thinkers. My opinion is that racism is a mental problem that has been around since this nation began. I've heard President Biden say so often that "there's nothing beyond our capacity as the United States of America." Nevertheless, throughout centuries, the problem of racism in many minds has continued.

According to (*World Book Encyclopedia, 1973, s.v."Psychology -History")*--"In the 1600's and 1700's some philosophers believed...the mind is empty at birth and that a person must have experiences to develop ideas."

The encyclopedia notes that Sigmund Freud (1856-1939) was an Austrian physician born of Jewish parents in Moravia. He was the first to map the unconscious world of the human mind. He fled to London to escape from the Nazis in 1938 and died the following year. Slavery, that *World Book Encyclopedia* called an evil system, was abolished in 1863 in the U.S. before Freud fled to London. He studied the mind and was a psychoanalyst and "taught that memories stored in the subconscious mind influenced a person's mental life." (*World Book Encyclopedia, 1973)*

Freud devoted himself to psychology--the science that studies all kinds of human behavior (normal and abnormal). *World Book Encyclopedia* added that psychologists deal with...

how we see, how we learn, and how we form attitudes. Perhaps racism could be studied. The encyclopedia further noted that 'the mind took up no space and couldn't be weighed, seen or touched." I did not research whether Freud delved into how the mind of a racist works.

After all these centuries of racism and knowing its harm as a Black grandparent, my wonder is why there has not been much change around this issue.

This pandemic of racism is especially rampant in the U.S. criminal justice system where a majority of those affected and being locked up in this pandemic riddled institution of racism called the criminal justice system are Blacks. Some have been entrapped for years and some for life. The false mindset of many seems to be if they're Black, they're up to something illegal.

Research notes that it's been "more than fifty years since President Nixon first declared this cruel War on Drugs. It has devastated families and communities across generations." *Drug Policy Alliance*, "End the Drug War and Undo its Harms," June 24, 2023, New York.

The criminal justice system is a corrupt racist institution that makes Blacks several times more likely to be arrested and put behind bars than whites. According to Manning Marable, "Blacks comprise over 25% of all Americans arrested in a given year" (Marable, 1983, 113). Although whites are charged with 72 percent of all criminal offenses, they're punished for certain less serious crimes.

In my opinion, more Black families are impacted because so many more young Blacks are targeted, arrested and put behind bars than any other group.

It seems that there will be no change to this situation with either a Republican or Democratic administration. Alexander reports that people of color are still being "disproportionately [put] behind bars since the first prisons opened", (Alexander 2020, 187).

In my research, I've concluded that the plan was always

a premeditated intent to continue capturing Blacks as the favorite whipping boys. To reiterate, "since the days of slavery, Black men have been depicted and understood as criminals and that so-called "criminal nature" has justified their treatment," (Alexander, 298). It was a crime for a slave to run away because that affected the slave owner's profit, a part of his livelihood, since the law said the slave was the massa's property. That's what police were appointed for early in the republic; to catch runaway slaves. Running away caused economic loss.

The criminal justice system in the twenty-first century is still an institution established and well-funded by the government, as was slavery. Millions and billions are voted on and legislated every year for the War on Drugs. It has replaced slavery, which similarly was funded for centuries to make a profit off the misery of others. Overwhelmingly now, this affects Black descendants of slaves from Africa, not from Sweden. That's what happened in slavery. It's in the criminal justice system where this pandemic, in my opinion, is the most unrestrained due to the War on Drugs. I would think that in no other budgeted department than prisons is there more racism from so many; judges, prosecutors, the police, and prison workers all direct their individual biases at the prisoners.

If your family has not been affected yet, you probably know (if you are Black) at least one young Black male (perhaps a friend) who has spent time in prison, been arrested, or has a criminal record. One can get a criminal record no matter how much or little time spent behind bars. You can easily get the prison label on your record if you are Black, because of the intense targeting of Blacks.

A criminal record means many things, but for Blacks it means the slave-master mentality is still alive and well. That mindset is still to keep as many Blacks as possible from rising from the lowest level of society, just as in colonial America. Law enforcement especially wants to give as many young Blacks a criminal record as they can to help keep the prison population up with their preferred prisoners. That also makes many more Blacks ineligible to vote, helping to suppress the Black vote. It is noted that, "about half of European countries allow all people behind bars to vote," (Alexander, 2020, 198).

In the War on Drugs, it's an unlevel playing field and unequally legislated racist justice. Young Blacks are put behind bars for the same crimes that are largely ignored when committed by whites. "Whites are consistently more likely to avoid prison and felony charges, even when they are repeat offenders. Black offenders, by contrast, are routinely labeled felons," (Alexander, 2010, 2012, 189). By avoiding prison many whites also avoid solitary confinement.

Crimes of murder, rape, grand theft, assault, and so on are different. Those kinds of violent crimes usually could trigger calls to 911 (for bodily harm) -- drug crimes are more consensual interactions, and they don't necessarily threaten physical harm.

If you are Black, you probably know at least one young Black who has experienced one of the scenarios mentioned above. Hopefully yours is a family that has been spared. Criminalization is a gross well-funded government atrocity that has happened to so many of our young Black men under the cover of the War on Drugs. All the legal discriminatory policies and laws against Black men are intended not only to affect that one individual: they're intended to affect their children too, who are innocent of any crime. They're intended to affect all those connected to the inmate who could also be innocent of any crime. I, an eighty-year-old grandparent, want to know what I've done to bring this torment on myself. We're having to deal with, according to Ephesians 6:12, "spiritual wickedness in high places" because of the color of our skin, even when up in age.

I ask again: did you know that almost half of all prisoners in the U.S. at any given time are Black? (Marable, 112). However, Blacks are only 14 percent of the U.S. population. That's just preposterous that in the U.S. almost half of all prisoners are descendants of slaves. Back to one in three, that's a wide net designed to snare as many Blacks as possible. The criminal justice system is operating to make young Black criminals. Fathom one third of any race having colorectal cancer. Prison is like giving all those young Black men a dreaded disease. It's deliberate because they still target Blacks.

I hope at least one Black family has been spared being snared in the criminal justice system due to the War on Drugs.

I see right through the schemes. Those who had the power had to create evil to make crime, to repeat, because violent crime was declining. They created the new program named the war on drugs, and made drug crimes mostly non-violent. "Until 1988, one year of imprisonment had been the maximum for possession of any amount of any drugs," (Alexander, 2010, 2012, 54). During President Reagan's administration, in 1988, Congress revisited a new mandatory minimum for drug offenses. It included establishing "a five-year mandatory minimum (sentence) for simple drug possession...even for first-time offenders", (Alexander, 2010, 2012, 53).

Accordingly, Alexander continues that the Reagan administration cut in half investigation for white-collar criminals. They were probably older, richer, and mostly white. His Justice Department "cut in half the number of specialists assigned to identify and prosecute [them]" (Alexander, 2010, 2011, 49). It shifted law enforcement resources, instead, "to street crime, especially drug law enforcement."

They then convicted more Blacks. In essence, the president wanted to prioritize drug law enforcement and shifted to mostly people of color (especially Blacks) who were less affluent and didn't have the money from white-collar jobs. Therefore, they would be less able to hire lawyers to defend themselves and would have to stay locked-up, helping increase the declining prison population.

I was a living witness at the time that Reagan advanced

the War on Drugs, which led to mass incarceration. He helped lay the groundwork: policies in his administration that made Blacks ten to fifty or sometimes 90 times more likely to be arrested in general and convicted for drug crimes than Whites in some states. In Reagan's administration, history shows that law enforcement was bribed to arrest as many as they could. These bribes helped to continue the overrepresentation of Blacks imprisoned. His polices helped fill up the prisons, plundering and pillaging much of the Black inheritance – our young men given to us from God first, but also depleted our capital trying to defend them. I think the president just didn't want to prosecute so many whites like himself. The result of these actions speaks for itself. Who was locked up? White-collar office crimes were also classified as non-violent, but investigation for them was cut, as already mentioned. Nonviolent drug crimes, which especially affected Black and Brown young men, were later changed to felonies from misdemeanors. With the stroke of a pen, the shift was made from investigating those office crimes to street crimes that filled up the prisons overwhelmingly with Blacks charged with non-violent drug crimes, while at the same time, non-violent office crimes were cut.

Just as unjust as slavery; however, this drug war continues to cause the breakup of families of color, especially Blacks. My loved one didn't hold his first-born child until after he was released. But as John Locke, a Puritan in the colonial era said back then -- he would still probably advise his believers to "feel nothing at all of other's misfortune [they're slaves]" (qtd. in Kendi, 49). Today, he'd say instead that they're young descendants of slaves. In my opinion, "to have no feelings about others' misfortune", is some weird grace Locke preached to his followers.

John Locke was also a statesman in government in colonial times. "He helped draw up the Carolinas Constitution," as Kendi reports (49). Another Puritan, Richard Baxter, preached that "slavery was just and should not be resisted" (Kendi, 48). Kendi further reports that "not many Englishmen were more knowledgeable—or less compassionate" than Locke about British Colonialism and slavery (Kendi, 49).

In my opinion, from my research, Locke's message was not very caring.

According to Alexander, "in the mid-1980s [the Reagan era], prison admissions for African-Americans…nearly quadrupled in 3 years." It increased steadily until 2000, when it reached the level of more than twenty-six times the level of 1982 when Reagan took office. All the imprisonment for descendants of slaves under Reagan just continued the overrepresentation of young Blacks as inmates and ex-felons as when prisons first opened (Alexander, 2020, 123) as also reported.

Just as runaway slaves were targets of police during slavery, their Black descendants are still targets now, but for drug offenses. Mass incarceration is just like slavery—a massive profit-making industry in the U.S. with young blacks now the preferred clientele. I think that the quadrupled admissions of Afro-Americans in three years during the Reagan era really advanced mass incarceration and was not a coincidence. To repeat, law enforcement prioritized drug crime but cut back on arrestees for white-collar crime. My wonder is why didn't they make the non-violent white-collar fancy office crime a felony? Non-violent white office crime was not made a felony like possession of illegal drugs. Law enforcement goes to the poorer, disadvantaged neighborhoods of color and handcuffs young descendants of slaves, just like in times past when slave traders went to Africa with chains to capture slaves.

Those incentives Reagan started for law enforcement should be stopped if they haven't been already. The people in power can and do make anything against the law (illegal) that they want and also change laws as they wish. They made marijuana illegal (the War on Drugs) and can change it. It was against the law to teach slaves to read centuries ago, but they changed that. They also threw out many cases in the lunch counter sit-ins. It seems that there are still many who want to keep Black folks' lives as similar to the times of slavery as they can with the War on Drugs. Just as in colonial America, many whites (but not all) still want to control, harm, or adversely affect as many Blacks as they can with barriers, locking them up and denying them freedom for the pursuit of happiness, just because they can.

According to Alexander (2020, 2012), "Many wonderful good-hearted white people…are generous to others, respectful to their neighbors, and even kind to [some Black people but believe] the time is not yet right for equality so young Black men can have happiness" with their own families (183). All those prisons have been built and I repeat, I think crimes were specifically created for the War on Drugs. Following that, a whole slew of laws was passed by some in power. These policies were then enforced primarily against young Blacks because so many White people still feel that it's not yet the right time for Blacks to have the same pursuit of happiness that they have. These laws, policies, and so on have been enforced primarily against young Black men to pay the big salaries of mostly white judges, white prosecutors, police, and others. There seems to be an unwavering, compulsive attitude among so many whites that young Black men need correction.

I feel so bad for all my Black brothers and sisters. As the book of Esther 8:6 said, "How can I endure to see all this evil that has come unto my people." That's how I feel—like Esther. However, unlike in Esther's situation, all this evil didn't just start. History notes that it's been happening for centuries. But as already stated, there are so many "good-hearted White people who are generous to others and even kind to some Black people, but don't believe it's yet, the right time for equality."

To repeat, research documents that when the first U.S. prisons were operated, Blacks were disproportionately represented. Now, modern legislators have changed since there are no more runaway slaves. In their place, they created the War on Drugs and made young Black men primarily the continued targets for arrest and incarceration for illegal drugs to take away their freedom, as in slavery. All of this is to make a profit, as in slavery, just because they can. No matter whether Republican or Democratic administrations are elected, the scenario of overwhelming young Blacks locked behind bars stays the same.

BLACKS IN COLONIAL AMERICA

To do due diligence in telling this story about my loved one, Sherman (he could be anyone's young Black loved one, son, grandson, nephew); I decided to start in colonial America. That's where Sherman's ancestors came from by way of slave ships from Africa. I'm starting in colonial America because it's my view that there are many young Blacks especially (other races too) who haven't read an account like this, even though much of this information is in the 1973 edition of the *World Book Encyclopedia*. Even with all the new phones, computers, and other devices, many still can't afford the monthly expense for that technology. If they can afford such a device, I wonder if there's that much information available on apps about colonial America, where many young descendants of slaves come from.

Being a trained librarian in the 1960s, I remember that encyclopedias were once the main source for accurate information. Now there's Google and other resources, but do they include information from times way back? The *World Book Encyclopedia* notes that early slaves were of all races— and at one time, conquerors simply killed their prisoners. However, things changed, and most slaves later in history were Negroes—Sherman's ancestors.

The *World Book Encyclopedia* defined slavery as a practice in which human beings own other human beings. It goes on to say that a slave works for his or her master or owner without pay. The *World Book Encyclopedia* continues that slavery in the United States began in the early 1600s. By 1860, there were about 3,954,000 Negro slaves. Most American slaves came from Africa, either voluntarily or against their will.

I will compare life in colonial America to Sherman's life as he grew up in the 2000s and show how they were very much alike. Many things are still the same. Research from the encyclopedia notes that back in early colonial times, many different kinds of people lived in the thirteen English colonies that became the United States. Even though most of the colonies were populated by English settlers, thousands of settlers were not English. Many settlers came to America because they were unhappy with life in their homelands. They wanted to make a better life in the New World.

The *World Book Encyclopedia* states that, some settlers received several hundreds of acres of free land from individuals or companies to develop. Because colonial America was the most democratic place in the world, members of lower classes (except slaves, Sherman's ancestors) could easily rise to a higher class. A free settler had several new opportunities in the New World and could choose from several lines of work. He could be a successful farmer, owner of a large estate, owner of livestock, a shopkeeper, a business owner, or a skilled worker who invested his money. Only slaves were limited and bound to spend their lives at the lowest level of society. Most could not move up. Most worked in Southern colonies as laborers or house servants in homes or shops. Slaves and their children remained slaves unless their masters freed them. They were prevented from rising to a higher class like European settlers because of the color of their skin.

That free land and the various opportunities to make a living were bootstraps for settlers' new starts. On the contrary, slaves mostly didn't have much opportunity for bootstraps. Yet some whites (but not all) said, "Pull yourself up by your own bootstraps." There were none in slave ships crossing the ocean. It seems that many whites have selective memory loss about all the things their ancestors did to hinder Blacks from having bootstraps. There were hindrances and barriers from both individual slave owners and from policies of municipalities.

History also tells us about George Fox (1621–1691), a religious leader in England who founded the Quakers. He was led by his spiritual experience to witness what Quakers felt was that "inner light," which should aid a person's conscience in guiding his or her faith and actions. The spiritual song "This Little Light of Mine" is still sung in many churches today all these many years later. Mr. Fox believed he had received a divine call as a young man and began preaching his ideas about that "inner light." *World Book Encyclopedia* goes on to report that Mr. Fox was imprisoned and publicly punished many times because of his religious belief. It's noted that Quakers were pioneers in removing barriers to racial equality and have been among the leaders in prison reform. Reverend Fox's work way back in the 1600s is similar to that of Reverend Doctor Martin Luther King in the 1900s. How much the world is the same.

To backtrack a bit, Sherman's earliest ancestors on his father's side lived on a small farm or plantation. It is said that after the Civil War, very few slaves owned property or made wills. The only records kept of them were the bills of sale from slave ship to plantation owners or from buyers of slaves. Much of what we know about our ancestors has been passed down by word of mouth from one generation to the next. Sherman's ancestors were supposedly freed through emancipation, but that freedom for many young Black men did not last. Sherman was free, but then put behind bars. Some of those who had power in the U.S. government just did an about-face regarding emancipation. They reversed their stance on the official legislature's determination that slavery was a wrong system sponsored by the government and maintained for centuries.

Many sons and daughters of former slave owners and others who had the reins of power now focus on taking away the freedom of young male descendants of slaves in order to keep the jail and prison population up. This is done to pay out all those big salaries to mostly white judges, white prosecutors, police, and others under the War on Drugs—a program similar to slavery in its intent to make a profit off the misery of mostly Blacks.

The early American colonies built those jails and houses of correction, I suppose, for most anyone awaiting trial. Today, they are being turned into places for punishment after conviction. They house overwhelmingly large numbers of descendants of slaves, but not as many young offspring of former slave traders and slave owners or other whites.

To divert for an instance, from my understanding, the phenomenon of mass incarceration did not happen in slavery. Of course there were horrors. It's only in recent decades since our government's creation of the War On Drugs, that that terminology has been in the news. Sherman's grandfather was born in 1892 after the slaves were freed in 1865. Thankfully, he did not have to deal with a program like the War on Drugs, mass incarceration when he was growing up.

Forecasting Sherman as an inmate, it seems that prisons in the U.S. were built to detain and punish Blacks from the beginning—especially young Black male descendants of slaves. Many of those in power seem to be bent on taking away the freedom of young Blacks.

I'm a living witness that President Reagan's administration did a lot to continue that trend that was started in the first prisons, namely, overrepresentation of Blacks in prison. He helped lay the groundwork to capture my loved one and countless other young descendants of slaves, who are also loved by someone. As already mentioned, in the mid-1980s (the Reagan era), "prison admissions for African Americans nearly quadrupled in three years" (Alexander, 2020, 123). That unjust, racist war on drugs that advanced so much under Reagan is still being greatly enforced. I call it unjust because Blacks are routinely selected and put behind bars while whites are ignored.

In Reagan's administration, law enforcement was bribed, and they arrested as many as they could in the drug war. The large number of arrests was done through sweeps in mostly poorer communities of color (especially Black), also known as "the hood." These financial incentives should be revoked if they have not been already. Since that bribery was not publicized very well, the public could have thought drug use was increasing in certain populations without realizing that law enforcement bribes could be helping fuel the war on drugs.

What is so noble about being paid to force with guns and other devices the capture of someone who hasn't done anything to you? From my understanding and insight on the War on Drugs, I view it as an unprovoked government offensive against its own citizens of color. Planning a war usually means maybe planning to take prisoners if necessary too. It is the young Blacks who have been captured as prisoners and locked up in unprecedented numbers in this drug war. The provocation seems to have stemmed from our ancestors trying to run away from being kidnapped as slaves. Some who claimed slaves were their ancestors' property might still be brooding about them running away.

As the scripture says in Micah 2:1,"Woe unto them that devise iniquity, and work evil upon their beds. When the morning is light, they practice it because it is in the power of their hand. They oppress a man and his house, even a man and his heritage." That's what's happening in the Black community because of the War on Drugs. If you are Black, it's impossible to not know what this drug war has done to our heritage. Our heritage is a large number of our young Black men—our gifts from God—locked behind bars. Those who have no connection to Blacks can get some information from TV.

In my studies, the reason why admissions for Afro-Americans

quadrupled (in the Reagan era), was, according to (Alexander, 2010, 2012, 49) that, "the Justice Department...cut in half the number of specialists assigned to identify and prosecute white-collar criminals. [Instead they shifted] to street crime, especially drug - law enforcement." From my analysis and further research and insight and visiting the prisons later, they arrested and convicted many more young Blacks (four times more). That quadrupled the number as Alexander reported. My view from reading is that these young blacks were mostly less affluent and didn't have white-collar jobs. More of the young, poorer Blacks would have to stay in jail, less able to hire lawyers than the more affluent white-collar criminals where numbers were cut. Therefore, more young Blacks would help add to and keep up the prison population that was in decline.

There were "drug sweeps and suspicionless stops and searches...in record numbers," (Alexander, 2010, 2011, 72), in the Reagan era. Unprecedented numbers of African Americans were "rounded up for non-violent drug offenses (72). Young Blacks were always the most targeted.

For that reason, I believe President Reagan has been the worst president for Blacks in my lifetime. I haven't uncovered where under any other administration Blacks' imprisoned increased four times more.

I feel tricked and betrayed at how in hindsight, the defense budget increase was so much. Then, our leaders switched and used so much of that defense increase against Blacks. They took away the freedom of so many Blacks, locking them up. President Reagan got permission to have the military help in drug arrests, while still targeting young Blacks. Blacks were not foreign invaders as in World War 1 and when Japan bombed Pearl Harbor. Blacks didn't have atomic bombs either.

I don't believe that quadrupling the prison admissions for African Americans in three years of the Reagan administration was a coincidence. A slew of laws, rules, regulations, and policies had to be put in place and carried out to make this happen. Though Blacks were supposedly freed through emancipation, that freedom, it seems, can be taken away. It has not lasted for unprecedented numbers of young Black males. The War on Drugs was concocted by those with power who did not want young Black male descendants of slaves to have freedom. Many are still bent on controlling Blacks -- capturing the young Black males now, as they did slaves way back then, to put them in jail to keep the prison population up. Prisons are a business that might now be nearly as profitable as slavery.

This country is still a racist country and a lot of those in power want to legislate some of the same practices from colonial times. You can't read the Bible without discovering that it includes ethics of how to behave toward other people. In colonial America, I'm sure our ancestors loved their children in spite of intolerable suffering and difficulties.

I believe that some here in the U.S. may have learned from the history about Hitler and that could have influenced their behavior towards Blacks here in the U.S. There's a lot of cruelty towards Blacks. The encyclopedia describes Hitler as one of the most evil men in world history. He ramped up atrocities in Europe toward Jews whereas President Lincoln tried to stop some of the wrong in America. Now, the War on Drugs is ramping up atrocities again against our young Black men. The criminal justice system are continuously making our young Blacks felons. The encyclopedia notes that as a boy, Hitler sang in the church choir, but as an adult he hated Christianity, which he said was a religion for weaklings. As a boy, he learned to hate non-Germans, especially Jews and slaves. Many ancestors of those here in the U.S. who came from Europe likewise, may have espoused some of the same ill-natured cruelties and atrocities as Hitler, but maybe just not to the same extreme. Hitler committed suicide.

A contrast is that some European settlers claimed to be helping convert the barbaric slaves to Christianity. But just as Hitler, many didn't practice or embrace Christian principles themselves with Christian action, and many still don't. Regarding many in law enforcement, it seems like some of the same hateful attitudes Hitler showed toward Jews seem to be the practice of many of our especially white law officers who take the oath to protect and defend, but maybe not defend if they're young Blacks. The large imprisonment numbers show that many Blacks are being arrested, not protected.

Considering the police, the prosecutors, the judges, and other court officials, they all work together—and mostly one will not intervene to contradict another enough to make a different outcome. In all their eyes, if one says the victim needs to be behind bars, they all mostly come to the same conclusion. Among them, there is not much difference today than what it was with a runaway slave. If a southern plantation owner said you were a slave and not free, you were a slave unless a white person interceded. But it's worse now because in a court of law, hardly any white person or officer will intercede on behalf of a young Black man. They all mostly close rank.

In compiling this part of the writing so far, (I repeat) that Kendi states that the settlers from Europe brought their racism to the U.S. Here especially, they made a better life enslaving Africans. Despite emancipation, as already mentioned, some leaders did an about-face and took away freedom of the pursuit of happiness, especially of young Blacks. President Reagan's administration advanced the War on Drugs. Still a racist country in almost every area and institution, under the cover of the War on Drugs, our leaders which include some prejudiced, flawed men, helped make laws and carried them out as if they were supreme as from the infallible God.

But as Dr. Martin Luther King said, some laws are bad in the first place. In my time, I've seen how legislators from time to time will revisit and change even their own laws. With the lunch counter sit-ins that I participated in, where many good people were jailed for breaking the law - most of these cases were thrown out.

In my view, many of the cases in the War on Drugs should be thrown out as many states have already decriminalized marijuana.

Navigation through the "pandemic of racism" in these United States of America can be a daunting task for many Afro-American students. That term "pandemic of racism" that I heard my pastor say, is the best way I can describe what many of our Black students face every day. However, there's no government entity assigned to study it and to try and find a remedy like with COVID-19.

CHAPTER 2

GROUNDWORK FOR MASS INCARCERATION

Starting school is really hard when young Blacks have to figure out how to navigate through these racist United States of America, where the rules can change without prior notice. Before starting elementary school, maybe some younger students don't even know how to say that long word *discrimination* that they're almost sure to experience along the journey. The entrapment pitfalls when older are not as many for young females as for young Black males. Many females will have a safety net (however weak): the welfare program if they have an early unexpected pregnancy. But I don't know of any such program for young Black males who routinely face unemployment.

For many young Black men, like Sherman in particular; the journey can be rough, different, and unpredictable leading to a diploma or no diploma, whatever comes next. I saw firsthand how the unavoidable entrapment process of those like Sherman began. It's still all a subtle, often camouflaged plan to keep young Blacks at the lowest level of society just as in slavery, which has been replaced with the War on Drugs where laws and policies of discrimination still abound. As a young Black male, legislated laws and polices made Sherman four times more likely than whites to be arrested for marijuana, as noted in the House's hearing on decriminalization of marijuana.

A few instances of additional reporting, according to (Alexander, 2010, 2012) regarding how many more times Black males are likely to be arrested than Whites follows. Five times more likely by the NYPD between 1997 and 2006, (136); thirteen times more likely to be admitted to state prison in general, (100); from twenty to fifty - seven times more likely than white men in fifteen states (98); About 90 percent of those sentenced to prison for a drug offense in Illinois are African Americans, (189); and so on depending on the state. Blacks are more likely to be arrested and sent to federal prison on illegal drug charges that many more times, as already mentioned, than whites.

Those who make the rules have stacked the deck so the government can win with laws and policies they themselves legislate and execute to entrap unprecedented numbers of people of color (especially Black), imprison them for however long or place them on probation or parole. There are all kinds of regulations and requirements to keep as many young Blacks as possible restrained, at the lowest level of society, just like in slavery – unable to rise.

I had not heard the phrase "from school to prison pipeline" until Sherman's journey led him to middle school, specifically sixth grade. I knew that the "zero tolerance" policy at this school was going to be bad for young black males because in a school disturbance, both students were punished. I can just imagine there was an internal gut feeling that the one who didn't start the disturbance had the right to defend himself. I was a teacher in the 1960s, in a kindergarten through twelfth grade school with a Black principal in a disadvantaged community. Our school had no such thing as in-school suspension and very little out-of-school suspension; there were study halls. Right away, I concluded that the "zero tolerance" policy at Sherman's new school in sixth grade was a deliberate, subtle disguise to feed the nation's prison complex with a guaranteed ready supply of young Black inmates who would already be conditioned to being punished in "zero tolerance."

It's a well-known fact that Black students are punished with suspension from school at much greater rates than whites. Most of the students suspended at Sherman's school were Black. Again as in the Bible (Micah 2:1), there are those who lie upon their ivory beds, and devise plans upon their beds to work evil. I imagine that someone decided that sixth grade was not too young to start priming young Blacks for warehousing, just not in cells yet. Perhaps someone did dream up making colonies in America and starting slavery. Now it's the evil racist War on Drugs program. I believe someone could have also dreamed it up and saw it as a program where they could make laws and policies and enforce them overwhelmingly on people of color, especially Blacks. That's what happened.

Genesis 6:5 states of humans that "every imagination of the thoughts of his heart was evil continually." Those plans from the Bible in the Book of Micah 2:1 are being carried out now. Unprecedented numbers of our young Black men—the heritage of our communities—are locked behind bars.

I wonder if a president may have dreamed up the War on Drugs that did so much damage to our communities, pillaging our heritage. According to (Alexander, 2010, 2011, 49), as already mentioned, President Reagan's administration cut in half investigation for white-collar criminals, who I imagine were probably mostly older and white and richer. My view is that he didn't want to prosecute so many whites like himself. It's noted that they did pass laws that were extraordinarily punitive on people convicted of drug crimes. They, as Alexander continues, prioritized drug law enforcement-and captured more people of color. At the same time, they cut back on capturing white-collar criminals. The young Blacks that they shifted to instead, were poorer and didn't have white-collar jobs.

To achieve the shift, resources had to be diverted from some serious crimes such as murder, rape, violent assault, and others. I think that in the War on Drugs, law enforcement is so busy arresting and convicting the more easily targeted young men of color for nonviolent drug crimes, that there's not as much attention on violent crime. They started locking up small-time offenders who wouldn't have gone to prison in the past – John F. Pfaff, *Locked In, the True Causes of Mass Incarceration and How to Achieve Real Reform* (Basic Books, 2017) 59. It's stated that "drug arrests and convictions for drug offenses...caused mass incarceration," (Alexander, 2010, 2012, 102). She goes on to note that the "War on Drugs...has been waged primarily against non-violent, low-level offenders in poor communities of color," (209). That's where they do sweeps. The crux of the matter seems to be the great obsession of many in this nation is about how to put bounds and limitations on Blacks.

In Reagan's presidency, the program that provides federal aid to law enforcement was revised. They started offering millions of dollars in federal aid to state and local law enforcement agencies willing to wage the war. They did sweeps in the hood, but as already reported, gave less priority to apprehending white-collar criminals. This signaled the opportunity to catch the younger, poorer Blacks instead, based on the perverted twisted law—that made nonviolent behavior a felony to justify locking up countless young Blacks, that's what happened. Alexander also reported, that the result was that in the mid-1980s, the Reagan era, prison admissions for African-Americans, as already mentioned, nearly quadrupled in three years. Those in power made that happen with laws and policies just because they could, just like in colonial times when great numbers of European settlers oppressed slaves from Africa just because they could.

Never having supported anyone in the criminal justice system before, there was a lot I didn't know. I'm sure there are many other Blacks trying to make sense of this deluge of our imprisoned young Black men because of biased law enforcement. Alexander noted that Blacks are not offending anymore; it's disparities in enforcement. To repeat, young

Black men are four times more likely to be convicted of marijuana possession than whites, as reported in the 2022 House's hearing to decriminalize marijuana. They are up to eighty or ninety times more likely than whites in some states to be sent to prison on drug charges. That's just clear, intentional, systemic biased law enforcement and unequal justice.

My opinion is they are trying to give as many young Blacks as possible, criminal records. They don't teach that much about the criminal justice system (especially about those biased enforcement polices) in school. They try to get new clientele and keep those they have like any other business. The American criminal justice system is about enlarging the nonwhite prison population with, especially, Blacks. To me, it seems that the primary role of the law enforcement concerning Blacks is not to protect and serve, but to see how many they can arrest. Our criminal justice system is broken. They measure success by the number of people they arrest. They especially want to keep the Black clientele…by probation, parole, or other means (Alexander 2020, 119). As already mentioned, I didn't know much about the criminal system. I just learned that the judge and the prosecutors are lawyers who act on behalf of the government.

From my view and findings, "the prosecutor [is the one] who determines who gets sent to prison and for how long," as (Pfaff, 59), reported. He also notes that the prosecutor is to do justice. States are "locking up small-time offenders who would not have gone to prison at all in the past" (59). Since the prosecutor has the main role in this, my real wonder is why the decision was made to start locking up people who would not have gone to prison in the past. How is that justice?

I believe it was a resurgence in the Reagan era to restrain Blacks as in slavery, by barring them from rising beyond a certain level. My analysis is that because crime was declining, "prosecutors [started] bringing more and more felony cases against a [smaller number of arrestees,]" as (Pfaff 73) stated.

"An arrest [that] would lead to a felony case grew from about one in three to about two in three," (73).

Prosecutors use their own discretion and there's little meaningful check on it, according to (Alexander 2010, 2012, 117), they are not required to follow the American Bar Association of practice. Thereby, their own standard of discretion is allowed to flourish. Many of them are white, and could have some of the same biases as the white masses, against Blacks. Alexander states that "much racial bias... operates unconsciously and automatically -- even among law enforcement officials genuinely committed to equal treatment under the law," (2010, 2012, 107).

My view is that the whips of slave owners and slave traders have merely changed hands in the 2000s. The whips are now the biased discretion of mostly white judges, white prosecutors, police, and so on toward young Black men—the descendants of slaves. They're still the most imprisoned in the War on Drugs that has replaced slavery. It seems there's always another program, practice, or scheme designed to keep Blacks restrained from rising above a certain level. That's what the criminal justice system is doing, in my opinion. Today, just like in colonial times, many of those in power are offspring of European settlers who were in the slave trade. They learned from their ancestors, and they're still trying to do as their ancestors did: Children live what they learn many times, whether it is love, hate, or indifference.

CHAPTER 3

DERAILING A BRIGHT FUTURE

SHERMAN'S LIFE STARTED WELL WITH THE LOVE AND SUPPORT FROM family and friends from both sides of his family. They had hopes and dreams just like many other families. Sherman's grandfather on his father's side had already passed away before Sherman was born, leaving his grandmother on his father's side a young widow. Sherman had one beloved papa on his mom's side. Everybody loved Sherman, just like most Black families love their children today. Sherman's family had lots of love but Sherman never had an allowance -- the same as many other Black children.

Racists are everywhere with their mission to hinder, stop, create barriers, and so on in whatever way and whenever they can, against whatever the desire is of Black folk. Although slavery was outlawed, many whites have not outlawed its practice in their own hearts. Sherman would have to find out how to navigate through this pandemic of racism in the hearts of these racists in the United States of America. No one wants to admit to being racist. You don't have to. Just be silent.

In spite of his family's history, Sherman had a promising, bright future. That was intentionally blocked through the intricate disguise of a monstrous, ill-natured history teacher in eleventh grade. Every child deserves a chance to dream of a better future, to be all that they can be. As the old African proverb goes and was so eloquently quoted and emphasized by Hillary Clinton, "It takes a village." I always considered teachers a part of the student's village: the village away from home.

To backtrack and fill in a bit, from the beginning, Sherman was just a normal, happy, energetic, inquisitive toddler who was into everything but had good potential and promise, as did many other young children. The family got him involved in early childhood learning programs, hardly in preparation for incarceration. Attending story hour at the public library once a week at age two gave him a positive and structured outing to look forward to. It helped in developing his positive self-motivation. But the nay-sayers were already planning for incarceration. That kind of positive experience would not be factored in their thinking for their purpose because he was Black. The nay-sayers were already building jails and plotting how to fill them to make the almighty dollar, from locking up whoever they could trick or coerce and entrap, targeting young Black men especially.

One day, the librarian read the delightful children's book entitled *The Pigs' Picnic* by Keiko Kasza during story hour, showing the pictures on each page. Suddenly, near the end of the story, Sherman jumped up, screaming, "That's him! That's him!" Sherman had figured out that it was Mr. Pig in disguise who had borrowed several things—a beautiful tail from the fox; and stripes and other things from animals he met along the way to Miss Pig's house. Mr. Pig wanted to look his best to impress Miss Pig to go on a picnic with him. But no, no, oh no! Miss Pig realized something wasn't right when Mr. Pig finally got to the house and knocked on the door.

Seeing the scary looking, disguised Mr. Pig, Miss Pig screamed, "Who is this monster?" She didn't recognize Mr. Pig. "If you don't leave, I'll call Mr. Pig and he'll take care of you." Sherman had figured out a disguise at age two that he understood. There would be other subtle, and more intricate, intentional disguises later in his growing years, journeying through the pandemic of racism that Sherman wouldn't be likely to unravel so easily.

After story hour, the librarian said that was the first time she'd experienced such an outburst when reading that story. At age two, Sherman was probably one of the youngest children in the group of varying ages. The nay-sayers were busy trying to plan negative traps for young Blacks. To the contrary, the librarian didn't show displeasure. Instead, she was caring and told Sherman she was glad he came to story hour that day. Sherman was getting very positive feedback in early learning. But as already mentioned, that would change later with a monstrous, ill-natured teacher in subtle disguise in eleventh grade with his subtle, hostile, negative feedback. It seemed that he derived sadistic pleasure from mistreating other young Blacks like my loved one.

In a few years, Sherman graduated from pre-school, where he was excited to read a book for the first time in front of the big crowd at the pre-school graduation ceremony. However, the nay-sayers were continuously plotting for the opposite path; prison, not education. He had already learned to read with the program his beloved papa had given them—hardly to prepare him for incarceration. On the other hand, some of our leaders don't value education, especially for Blacks. They don't want to acknowledge and accentuate positives in many young Blacks who show potential. Instead, they're cutting education budgets but finding millions and billions to build steel prisons, anticipating more criminals to be put behind bars, all while intentionally targeting young Black males.

They concocted the War on Drugs and made crimes for it to fulfill a whole one-track-mindset; to build prisons with my tax dollars and capture large numbers of my people to put behind bars. They chase that almighty dollar, creating misery for Blacks and making them prisoners for profit. You can see for yourselves who is locked up. Our government leaders would rather allocate billions to make young Blacks prisoners, as they are doing, rather than invest in making them scholars to be all that they can be. According to (Alexander, 2010, 2012, 190) "young Black men are more likely to go to prison, than to college in Chicago". That's also true in many cities across the nation. To repeat, as Marable has said, "almost half of all prisoners at any one given time in the U.S. are Black," Manning Marable, *How Capitalism Underdeveloped Black America (Haymarket Books, 1983)* 112. First, those in power captured slaves with chains, weapons, and brute force for profit. Now, they use guns and handcuffs in the War on Drugs, which has replaced slavery. What is the great, noble, and just reason for the War on Drugs?

Going back to Sherman's journey, he was still young, still excited, and highly motivated. He started kindergarten and loved it. Early in the year, an unfortunate thing happened in the family; a broken home. I resigned myself to be a more helpful part of the village that Hillary Clinton often spoke about. I went to the family home more often. Sherman appeared to continue developing with good confidence, always making good grades, and he seemed happy. I don't even know if he knew what prison was. In kindergarten, his teacher recognized Sherman's natural potential and good character -- contrary to the nay-sayers building prisons with Sherman and other young Blacks already in mind. By third grade, the nay-sayers would evaluate these young children to determine how many prisons to build by the numbers of slow readers. The nay-sayers were predicting that these young Black males would do nothing useful in life if they didn't read well by third grade.

But in third grade, Sherman had an African-American teacher named Mrs. Will, who he later in middle school identified as his favorite teacher. She really made a positive impact on Sherman. She showed sincere concern and encouraged him to be the best he could be. I don't know if Mrs. Will was his first African-American teacher, but even young children can tell when a person sincerely cares about them. A teacher can hardly fake sincere care and unwavering concern, but I feel that sincere concern is lacking in many whites (but not all) who teach Black students. It's so important to see someone like yourself.

As an educator and grandparent, I was doubly dedicated to helping my grandchildren be successful, just like I did for my own children. Sherman knew them and aspired for the same good life beyond high school. He loved comradery and would share writing and reading, vocabulary, and spelling assignments with me from Mrs. Will's class. She helped him feel proud to achieve. He would ask to read some of the stories he wrote in Mrs. Wills's class to me. I was proud that he found me interested in his work and wanted me to be involved with his learning. Mrs. Will was seemingly both perceptive and empathetic. She was really interested in the whole child, both in and out of school.

In sixth grade, things changed. Sherman continued to do well, but at this point along the journey, navigating through the pandemic of racism became more treacherous. There were policies I'd never heard of in the elementary grades. "Zero tolerance" was one of them. Early on, much of my talk with Sherman was about what zero tolerance was, so I knew this was strong on his mind. If your child was hit by another student, your child was not supposed to hit back. Both students would be suspended. However, Sherman had been taught to defend himself; if someone hit him, he hit back. He told me he knew students who were beat up because they didn't fight back. Sherman was never in a fight or sent to detention in grade school. In middle school, some students would tease him and some would try to test their strength on him because of his size. The zero tolerance policy was for both students to be punished with suspension.

Authorities in some schools like Sherman's adopted the zero tolerance policy, I repeat, that features punishment by suspension and expulsion. That's a precursor to taking away a student's freedom to learn, which leads to warehousing later. This brings me to inequities generated from racism in many areas.

It's racism that's behind Blacks always being targeted since slaves ran away in slavery. The idea that Blacks can't have the same pursuit of happiness as Whites is still in the minds and practices of many Whites. Just as it was illegal to drink water from the fountain for Whites only, a minor thing like following orders in school that seemed like a biased order to a student, can become a crime like a slave running away.

According to the ACLU, Black students [today in 2023] get higher legal punishment. In the 2017-18 school year… in this state that the ALCU reported on-law enforcement resource officers and school staff referred Blacks to law enforcement agencies 2.4 times as often as they referred White students, (Emily Walkenhurst, "student racial developmental disparities", WRAL.com). In my opinion, the same thing is probably happening in states across the nation.

The report states that suspensions and expulsions have for decades been disproportionately used against students of color and students with disabilities. This report just tells me that those in power intend to keep supporting mass incarceration, and targeting young Blacks like my loved one as feeders for the criminal justice system.

According to the report, Blacks are [made liable] for disorderly conduct, which can be minor offenses, four times more often than White students. Things like not following orders and cussing in the hallways can be the beginning of a criminal record in such a referral to school resource law officers. Seemingly, there's no limitation on what conduct might be construed as disorder. In my opinion, that's all subjective anyway as related to the construction of the mind of the individual law officer or staff personnel toward the student.

What about the open-mindedness, impartiality, tolerable or biased thinking of these school personnel.

The report says that some research suggests that Black students are disciplined more often for behavior as defiance. A Black student's refusal, to immediately do as asked by a school officer can automatically denote that that student feels that a crime is automatically being implied to him or her.

I repeat, as Michelle Alexander reported, "since the days of slavery Black men have been depicted and understood as criminals, " having a criminal nature, (2020, 298) because of trying to run away from the horrors of slavery. Descendants of slaves now, are still targeted.

There's always been a focus by some on punishment of Blacks for illegal practices-drinking water out of the fountain for White's only. You can never tell what the next flimsy illegal act will be. In the schools, educators end up turning to officers to handle student behavior, especially with limited social workers and counselors.

Back to Sherman in middle school, I continued as an essential part of the village to help Sherman and his two siblings grow up as normally as possible despite a broken home. Neither Sherman's dad nor I, had had to adjust to such a trauma when we were growing up. Another big difference was I went to school when segregation was the law of the land. All our teachers were Black (with no racist hang-ups). They wanted all their students to succeed and do well, and did not want to keep some of them down. There was no discrimination from teachers or students.

There was one thing I did not feel good about right away at Sherman's middle school; his enrollment in a class called Enrichment. Being Black, I sensed trepidation vibes when I could not determine the class's purpose from the name. Sherman already had language arts. The enrichment teacher did not attend open house for the sixth graders, where we met all his other teachers at the first of the year. That absence gave me bad vibes again following the vague class' name. Of course, as time passed, this was the first class where we needed to contact the teacher. Sherman had received an F, and he said he didn't know why. This was the first F he'd ever received for the end of the quarter grade. Having been a fair-minded and caring former Afro-American teacher myself, I didn't give a failing grade without first giving the student a chance to do extra work to improve. Without a call from school, I concluded that this teacher just didn't feel it worth her time to call. My gut feeling was right. When we met her, I saw she was an older Caucasian woman.

Sherman's dad was very busy with the other children and their needs and working full-time. As an essential part of the village, I took it upon myself to request the meeting, which was very hard to get. After making many, many calls and waiting many days with no return call, I finally looked in the phone directory and called the office for Student Services at the main school complex and reported our situation. Sherman's principal finally called me and a meeting was scheduled.

At the first meeting going back to Sherman in Middle School, Sherman's teacher said she had no answer to my question about "why no one called to let us know he was failing?" I already felt she didn't care because Sherman was Black or she just didn't care about teaching. She said Sherman "sat back there with all the others, who probably needed remedial" (help for someone having difficulty in a subject). Right then, I knew that with that kind of attitude, she felt because Sherman was Black, he would automatically have difficulty. However, after the meeting with Sherman's team, she became a good partner in Sherman's learning. I wondered about all the other children who might not have advocates like Sherman's. I wondered just how pervasive that kind of attitude was with all the Caucasians teaching Blacks, trying to impede their learning. I just happened to have time to investigate.

Sherman had always liked school, but I wondered about

this kind of teacher coupled with suspensions too. (Nay-sayers were plotting to exploit this kind of situation.) The assignment to write his autobiography in Language Arts class in sixth grade gave Sherman pause at first. But after encouragement and pointers, he wanted to write it and was very proud of his finished work. It turned out to be twenty-one pages of narrative and pictures. The teacher complimented Sherman for a job well-done and had him present it to all of her classes.

Sherman said his pet peeve was when someone accused him of something he didn't do. Another was being yelled at about something and it turns out that the other person was wrong. His ideal was a school with challenging classes and fun teachers. He added that he wished his family wouldn't be so affected by the economic struggle and that he could have an allowance. His dream was to earn a doctorate so he could get whatever job he wanted and be able to hold a job, and have a nice house. There was nothing villainous. Most villains are not interested in challenging classes or a doctorate. Again, (nay-sayers try to crush and hinder that type of focus in a black child.) But his Black language arts teacher in middle school had also brought out Sherman's potential and character as many others before. However, to the contrary, the nay-sayers were instead funding entrapment policies for incarceration.

Law enforcement with power and authority was only interested in finding one negative that they could figure out to make a crime, (like drinking out of the wrong water fountain) and capture Sherman. That is some of their master plan for Blacks, no matter their potential or character. One mistake erases everything good you've done often, if you're a Black young man. Many whites want to deemphasize that a young Black has potential and character but instead focus more on building jails and prisons for them. Anyone today can see the premeditated intent for who to put behind bars. To repeat, it was always the plan to capture Black and Brown young men as "the favorite whipping boys." "Since the days of slavery, Black men have been depicted and understood as criminals," (Alexander, 2020, 298). That's what many whites call the Blacks' "criminal nature." They were criminal because of trying to run away from slavery. Who wouldn't want to escape the horror of slavery? That personal understanding and attitude of ingrained, scornful resentment has been used to justify treating Blacks as criminals.

Police were appointed to catch runaway slaves early in the Republic. Nothing much has changed. Millions and billions are still allocated in the budget for the War on Drugs, just as slavery was well-funded. Making high profits off the misery of overwhelmingly young Blacks is still one of the highest priorities, just as slavery was.

None of the things Sherman accomplished in school (where the young spend a lot of time) point to being a villain. My opinion is that zero tolerance in middle school is the beginning of systematically punishing young Black students with suspensions to get them used to being warehoused -- just not in cells yet. At the end of sixth grade, Sherman gave a speech at the high school. The speech was on "Raising the Achievement of African American Males," hardly a topic of interest for a wanna-be villain. Afterward, the principal praised Sherman and said his speech was the best one. In the speech, Sherman said we need teachers who believe we can learn, saying "thank you to all the teachers that have helped and encouraged me." To those who prejudged him by negative stereotypes, to take a cue from Obama, "Yes we can." Yes I can. Nay-sayers ignore that kind of confident attitude in young Blacks. They think and plan prisons instead, thinking punishment because it's a Black child.

Along the journey navigating through all the racism where anything might happen, Sherman had learned how to recognize when he was being prejudged by biases. I noticed that more teachers showed biases in middle school than in Sherman's elementary school. I still wonder why.

Juxtaposed with Sherman's good "speech" and other good factors, I believe around the same time there was a scenario with Sherman's keys. That also ended in suspension, which to me seemed far-fetched and an overreach. A boy sitting in Sherman's group erratically snatched Sherman's keys off the desk for whatever reason. Sherman said he raised his hand to report it and the white teacher said "put your hand down." Sherman saw the teacher wasn't going to do anything. If she had acknowledged Sherman's hand, the deviant-thinking, playful student may have given the keys back. Without knowing why Sherman raised his hand, she didn't even try to do anything. Sherman needed his keys before going to the bus to let himself in at home, so he snatched his keys back. To repeat, he saw the teacher wasn't doing anything. It seems that some teachers might feel that zero tolerance absolves them from knowing anything besides their subject. There was no hitting, but the zero-tolerance policy was punishment of both students with suspension for the class disturbance. The other student said when both were sent to the principal's office that he was just playing and was going to give the keys back. Who knows what was in the mind of that erratic student?

Moving along, I called the school and asked, "What was the specific thing Sherman did that caused his suspension?" I don't think the administrator saw what happened in the classroom yet he said; "The boys were playing with the keychain." Perhaps the teacher had told him that, but in my opinion, this was not playing to Sherman. The erratic acting boy was the instigator and snatched Sherman's keys off the desk. Sherman needed them to let himself in at home and this was his last class. This was not a game.

My opinion as an educator with many years teaching in public schools is this: I believe that the "zero tolerance" experience gives cover and provides a license (the initiative) for a student like this with deviant, playful thinking to act it out if he or she wants to. They know the other student as well as themselves will be punished. My opinion is that punishing both students with suspension is just a well-thought-out ploy to condition all Black students to get used to possibly being punished for prison later. Zero tolerance provides no good learning or corrective principle. Basically, what I saw as the student's take away and internalization was "I was punished and just have to accept it," conditioning for acceptance of warehousing later.

The student with the deviant, erratic thinking is labeled as bad but so was my loved one, the victim of the erratic behavior, for responding. The message to take away is that one student is just as bad as the other and both just as responsible for the class disturbance. For responding, the victim is made to seem to have the same erratic behavior. Why else would both students be punished with suspension? Zero tolerance is just a ploy to say (as many Whites feel anyway), that all young Blacks are bad. That's far from the truth.

The scenario with Sherman's keys and how it all played out is a good example of how the "zero tolerance" policy makes both students equally responsible for the disturbance and treats both of them as bad with suspension, as if intentionally both of them were erratic in thinking and behaving from the beginning. Why else would they suspend both of them? To the contrary, the real world is supposed to be what school is preparing students for. Kyle Rittenhouse claimed self-defense. He killed two people with a rifle and wounded one other. With the judge's discretion, he didn't get any prison time. But zero tolerance in school in this instance doesn't mimic the real world, so what principle were they trying to teach?

Still alarmed and disappointed at the situation with Sherman, I reported it to someone else. The way the incident was handled just seemed unfair to Sherman. In the end, there was validation that the way it was handled was wrong. The school administrator said Sherman didn't tell him he raised his hand to report this to the teacher. I don't know if he did or did not tell the administrator he raisedd his hand, neither was the administrator in the classroom to see if he did. However, the administrator said; it would not have been right for the teacher not to acknowledge Sherman trying to report a wrong that happened to him. In my opinion, the administrator should have asked the teacher why she told Sherman to put his hand down. I had told the administrator, myself, what Sherman told me; the teacher said, "Put your hand down." But I don't know if any other conversation took place. School was out now for the summer.

I wrote the head principal and suggested that she write the teacher up and put in her folder how she contributed to one more suspension in Sherman's record because of her negligence. I don't know if the principal did that because I did not receive a response from her. In the meantime, another administrator at the main school service center told me he didn't think this incident with Sherman's keys was an infraction that needed to be handled through suspension. It seemed to me that how to handle a disturbance under zero tolerance could be subjective to whatever biased thinking or whim of the teacher or administrator. It is important to not lose sight of the principle you want to convey. What did both students take away in the end?

Students don't just learn math and reading at school. Sherman finished middle school in spite of all the distractions -- and still had a desire to get a college degree and be all that he could be. I don't know if middle schools with predominately white student enrollment had the zero-tolerance policy like Sherman's predominately Black school. What I do know, from working in both, is that a different, more compassionate better way of doing things is often in place at schools with a predominately white enrollment.

High School: The Last Year

Another part of the journey through the pandemic of racism began for Sherman. He started ninth grade with high hopes and strong determination. He played football too but had to transfer. It was to a school with more affluent students and a predominately white enrollment. Sherman played football there too, but he had to adjust to many new things. He was in a blended family with two more male teenagers at home and a new stepmom. He was not seeing old friends from church and his old neighborhood where he'd lived since birth. At school, for the first time; Sherman was one among a few African-American students. I hoped his teachers would be professional and genuinely, inclusively caring. However, I knew some of the things I'd had to deal with in a similar setting could cause some uneasy moments.

To repeat, I viewed teachers as a part of a student's village. My role as an essential part of the village changed some at the new school. I still helped with transportation to and from school, to football practice sometimes, to work, and so on. With all the new adjustments, including dealing with many who thought he didn't belong and wasn't welcome because he was Black, I'm sure being at this new school wasn't exactly a walk in the park for Sherman.

Eleventh grade was the worst part of navigating through this horrible pandemic of racism at that school. Sherman was trying to work more and still make good grades, anticipating buying a car and going to the prom. Knowing all this, I advised Sherman to take the regular history class instead of honors. He took my advice, but later in the year, I learned that the teacher moved Sherman from the regular class to honors because the teacher said he was doing so well in the regular class. Sherman had already told me he'd rather get an A or B in a regular class than a D or F in an honors class. I would too.

This situation as it unfolded reminded me of the fable

"Chanticleer and the Fox." The fox told the rooster how beautifully he could sing, but the fox had something sinister planned, as did Sherman's history teacher, who turned out to be a strong stalwart nay-sayer. Chanticleer threw his head back, closed his eyes, and sang at the top of his voice. The fox grabbed the rooster and ate him. Likewise, the history teacher said Sherman was doing so well in his regular class and moved Sherman to the honors class. This move probably appeared to Sherman like the teacher was trying to place him in a better opportunity. On the contrary, in a sinister disguise, this move put the onus on Sherman to have to catch up in a more rigorous class that had already started two months earlier and still do well. Perhaps as the rooster, Sherman didn't give it a second thought; he'd always done well. I don't know if the teacher had asked Sherman about the move first. It was mid-June before I learned Sherman had been moved from the regular class that I advised him to take.

Thinking back, it all unfolded to me now, the racist trickery. I only knew Sherman's grades had changed. I had taken him to get supplemental work as he said the teacher suggested before I knew about the move. That's what I had done in the lower grades and had also done for my own, now grown, children. Some of the specific aids that Sherman wanted were not available at the store the teacher suggested.

Having always been Black and now still an intelligent Black Afro-American and former teacher, my gut and insight were highly triggered. This white teacher had been up to mischief all along to keep from giving this young Black male an A or B in the first place. The teacher mischievously knew the move would put a heavier burden on Sherman, as already mentioned. There are white teachers like that who don't think Blacks should be on par with white students and will go to great lengths to try to prove it.

In disguise, the teacher used this camouflage of flattery to express his bias, just as was done to many slaves in colonial

America through different shenanigans. The teacher did this just as other racists, because he could. He had an inner malicious intent from his racist thinking—one of the basic widespread mental traits in the "pandemic of racism." To my disgust, but not to my surprise, Sherman was the first among my loved ones that I knew of whose journey navigating through school was so harsh, the teacher's nay-saying was continually vague. It can be hard to decipher the subtleties since many schools and classrooms are not very accessible during class time to parents who have to work. It was subtle; the teacher just did not have the village concern for fairness for Sherman because he is Black.

Sherman was young, inexperienced, and innocently open-minded. I'm not certain that he recognized the myriad of subtle, racist shenanigans yet. He didn't know the measures some whites would go to keep a Black male down, especially one who showed promise. His maternal white grandmother loved him, so he genuinely accepted whites. The teacher just had no respect for Sherman's ability. He wanted to try to keep Sherman at the lowest level of society as a slave if he could, to keep him from rising to another level.

Being challenged with technology, I was not able to help Sherman as much at this school. The system had changed from report cards and one had to know how to use the internet to access grades, which I couldn't do. I realized that in spite of my best efforts, some of the racist master plan followers are being paid my tax dollars to teach and show concern but instead are busy hindering, impeding, and blocking even our youngest Black students, both unconsciously and consciously. Just like when at their racist whims, they made a law against teaching slaves to read long ago, this history teacher is trying to do some of the same things in the 2000s; deter and delay or thwart learning.

Surely, this teacher was well-trained to be at that school. To be in education, he had to have had some learning in psychology. President Clinton said, "Your mind is your greatest asset." Most teachers choose teaching because they have a strong inner desire to do that. It is noble work. Teachers help develop the brain. From birth, the brain receives messages through the eyes, ears, and other senses that tell us what is going on in the world around us. Through the brain, we develop emotions. Fear, anger, hate, love, and indifference - all begin in the brain. From receiving all these messages, the person forms varied thoughts and reactions. This history teacher's indifference and hate began in his brain.

In my opinion, and as a former caring educator, I knew that a part of the history teacher's mission was to enhance, encourage, and help grow Sherman's knowledge, to inspire and help him improve. I did not see any of that from this teacher. By eleventh grade, Sherman already knew what he wanted in life: a doctorate. There was nothing villainous about that, though it was contrary to the nay-sayers planning prison for Sherman. This history teacher possessed an evil eye and an ill nature toward young Blacks, just like the European settlers toward slaves in colonial America.

In my only son's preschool class; he was the only Black in the class. His teacher told me that there was one thing she would not tolerate; for one child to knock down another child's blocks or whatever he or she was building. Perhaps she had seen this behavior in her class. However, this was a grown-up white history teacher who had probably never been taught any differently. Maybe like Hitler, he had learned Christianity but hated it. This teacher destroyed the good GPA Sherman had built up all along his journey navigating through the pandemic of racism in our schools. It was like the teacher was angry and took a sledgehammer to Sherman's work. It seems he discounted the family's investment in helping Sherman succeed.

Moving on, the damage had already been done, and I didn't find all this out until mid-June. This was, metaphorically speaking, like the narrowest water channel Sherman had to pass through. This narrow-minded, malicious history teacher put a blockage there just because he could, like all this was a game to him. I was very angry and met with the principal about how a good student was just allowed to fall through the cracks. The answer to myself was that this teacher was (as so many are these days) a subtle, full-time recruiter for the "from school to prison pipeline." Blocking good goals is one of the recruitment strategies. No one I talked to could find out the grade Sherman was given for the first semester when the teacher said Sherman was doing so well. That was the misleading reason the teacher gave for moving Sherman in the first place. He was really trying to cover up his actual bias.

I wondered what allowance the teacher made for the two months of work Sherman had missed in the honors class before moving him. As a former teacher, I knew the final grade could count heavily -- (sometimes the final test grade is the final grade). Sherman made a 71 as the final grade. That was a D or F, just what Sherman had said he did not want to happen. I wondered how and if the first semester grade, when the teacher said Sherman was doing so well, was factored into the final grade. How much assistance did the teacher give to help Sherman catch up for the two months of work Sherman missed before the move?

This history teacher, with all his shenanigans, had zero concern, if he even knew, that Sherman was working forty hours a week, taking the city bus, getting home from work often at eleven or twelve at night, and taking a full load of classes.

Added to all Sherman was trying to do, the unpredictable happened. The only beloved Papa Sherman had ever known, had a heart attack and passed away suddenly in Sherman's last quarter in eleventh grade during preparations for finals. I don't know if any of Sherman's teachers showed any more concern or support or allowed extra time if needed for Sherman to do make up work.

This was surely a very stressful and deeply hurtful time for Sherman. He missed several days of school. If the history teacher had not moved Sherman from the regular class that I had advised him to take, the load would have been more manageable, especially with his papa's sudden unexpected death. Sherman would have benefited from having the less rigorous class that I had advised him to take. My view, based on some of my experiences, is that racist teachers have no genuine concern for Blacks. They just don't care about anything about Blacks unless there's the almighty dollar with it. This history teacher didn't care to help academically, morally, or justly. He was a strong, willing carrier in the pandemic of racism—and spreading it at this school.

Ironically, this one history class in the last quarter of Sherman's junior year made him ineligible for acceptance at historically Black colleges and universities (HBCUs) and public colleges. The teacher ran out the clock for Sherman to apply to any other place, even out of state. To add insult to all that, the honors history class was a class I don't think was necessary for the possible career of Sherman's choice (math). He had demonstrated aptitude, strong ability, and strong interest in math, and may have been considering further studies in math or a related area.

It's also ironic because of the extra devious manipulative procedure available to the history teacher that he used to block Sherman. I'm thinking this could have been the very type of scenario for which HBCUs were established in the first place— unfair treatment, barriers, and other varied shenanigans used to try to trick and hinder Blacks in the past. To attempt to try to deny that Blacks are capable and deserving in the twenty-first century is analogous to making it illegal to teach slaves to read centuries ago. It is still happening today.

According to Marable, "less than 10 percent of all former

slaves in 1865 were literate" (193). Fast forward to the twentieth century, Black students demanded Black Studies to know their history.

It's notable how Governor George Wallace in the 1960s saw Blacks' desire for access to the schoolhouse as a threat to the preservation of white supremacy. Some whites still don't want greater recognition for our work. They want their conservative teaching to remain predominate (uppermost in importance). There's a resurgence of the false attitude that "Negroes had no history." That history has been a continued struggle in the face of adversity. Some still want to suppress it.

There's a resurgence of the past attempt to deny educational opportunity (dismantling affirmative action). "The forces of Jim Crow sought to prevent black people from achieving" in the past (Alexander, 2010, 2012, 213). Dr. Carla Hayden, the first Black librarian to be appointed as Librarian of Congress by President Obama said on a TV program in April 2023 that "an illiterate crowd is the easiest to rule." To my way of thinking that's why the slaveholders made it illegal to teach slaves to read ages ago. In varied ways, some leaders are still trying to deny educational opportunity by dismantling affirmative action and banning books – still in the 2000s.

Back to Sherman, many students wanted AP and honors classes because they would help their chances of going to an Ivy League school, as many of them aspire. But Sherman aspired for an HBCU education, like many of his family. He could see that they earned degrees and got good jobs. I also knew that over 50 percent of African-American professionals in the U.S. graduated from HBCUs. To the contrary, I knew many Black students these days, who started at predominantly white universities, dropped out and didn't graduate and instead ended up with a lot of debt.

Sherman was harassed too at this high school. A math teacher called Sherman's dad and said he believed Sherman cheated on a test and wanted Sherman to retake it. Sherman refused. He knew that he knew what he knew. Many have the position but don't want to help Blacks be all that he or she can be.

I think an oath of declaration for teachers in K through twelve stating a pledge to help all students be all that they can be (similar to the Hypocratic Oath) is appropriate. Parents too, should feel free to ask personnel what they're doing to help their individual child be all that they can be.

At schools prior to this one, Sherman was always encouraged and helped to achieve. The history teacher was a far cry from the interest Sherman's first Black teacher in third grade showed, and his white middle school principal. To repeat, this history teacher's action, to me, was tantamount to taking a sledgehammer to all the determination and planning his family and the village had helped Sherman build. That meant nothing to the nay-sayers building prisons either. Sherman is Black. Many believe Blacks will do nothing useful in life.

Sherman told me that a white teacher said to him one day, "I'm getting paid for what I do here. What are you getting out of this?" To me, she just wanted to be scornful and flaunt her white privilege. I don't think she was one of Sherman's teachers. The history teacher, however, had the power to help make Sherman another successful young Black man. However, he did not want Blacks to be successful and placed a stumbling block instead in Sherman's path. A few years after Sherman's graduation from the school he transferred to for twelfth grade, I learned that the school system had created a new office. At last, students so adversely affected by unfair teacher treatment (especially racists) could complain and maybe get some type of resolution. This office was created one year too late to affect Sherman without a rather involved process. I think that, with all the pervading racism, such a responsibility should be from someone designated in the U.S Department of Education. That would be appropriate.

Sherman was having to deal with what I didn't experience until after I had received my first degree and had had many years of successful employment as an educator. This history teacher blocked Sherman from even a first degree. That's what's happening now. Many of those with authority would rather plan for incarceration than help make plans to inspire and guide a Black student to be all that he or she can be.

I knew how some white professors tried to take away or change what I had earned and deserved. It's so unfortunate that this is happening in the early grades now. Because of my experience, we sent all of our own children to HBCUs. It is very disheartening to know that so many whites are allowed to do these kinds of things.

Sherman must have been angry. He didn't talk about a doctorate anymore. I think this history teacher had discouraged him so. I'm not sure if Sherman understood the deliberate, disguised, subtle process that had happened to him. Sherman was not a complainer. He usually tried to handle adversity the best way he could. He didn't talk about being discouraged. Sherman weighed his possibilities and made the wise decision not to stay at this racist school for his senior year. He saw the writing on the wall and didn't take a chance on more shenanigans, maybe even denial of a diploma after twelve years of mostly good achievement.

Senator Raphael Warnock, who grew up in Georgia, said in campaign literature that he "knew what it's like to be counted out before you even get started," (Warnock for Georgia, Washington, D.C.). This history teacher could see in Sherman's files that Sherman had made a good start. The teacher's platform and his evil spirit made him place a stumbling block in Sherman's path, just as in colonial America, because he could. As Senator Warnock might say, this history teacher counted Sherman out after he got started. Senator Warnock also stated on the program (CAP-Center for American Progress-Ideas) on C-Span Thursday 10/26/23. "All have something in our record we are not proud of but none of us want to be judged permanently by our worst mistake."

That's what is happening to so many of our young Black men like my loved one, Sherman. Their crime, a felony, will always be on their record, even from the unjust, racist War on Drugs.

Perhaps this teacher had never heard anything like Zechariah 8:17, "Let none of you imagine evil in your heart against his neighbor," or Romans 13:9–10, "Thou shalt love thy neighbor as thyself: love worketh no ill to his neighbor." It's a choice to do evil. When God made humans, he didn't make puppets. He gave them free will to make choices. God knows the hearts of all people. Evil in the world comes from an evil heart and an evil will or on the other hand, this teacher may have been like Hitler in that he learned Christianity but had an evil eye and chose not to practice it like many, especially some whites towards blacks.

I now realize that this experience with the history teacher was only a preview of things to come. I hadn't realized that Sherman would be encountering the same mindset that slave owners had in colonial America. Many of the masses of whites (but not all) still feel that their mission toward young Blacks is the same as those in the New World toward slaves—set up barriers, hinder, interfere with, or stop whatever Blacks are seeking, the same as the ole massa's attitude way back then, which was to maintain slavery. My opinion is that attitude now is to maintain the status quo, which is the War on Drugs.

As you followed Sherman's journey navigating through horrible racism in the school system, you saw that it started with hardly any incidents in elementary school. In my view, the "zero tolerance" program that began in middle school works in conjunction with the "from school to prison pipeline," which was just a slogan at first but became a fulfilling prophecy. It was promoted through building prisons and showing mostly blacks committing drug crimes on TV. At the same time, this kept the slogan in the forefront of students' thoughts.

As already mentioned, in my opinion, all the punishment (the core feature of the zero tolerance program) was just a ploy to gradually get students used to being warehoused and thinking about themselves as bad young Black people. Meanwhile, some legislators themselves were still busy making policies, and laws to support and possibly build more prisons for "someone."

According to (Alexander, 2010, 2012, 208) the War on Drugs was "a war declared with Blacks in mind." I agree. That's why law enforcement went almost exclusively to poor communities of color rather than to white suburban communities. That's just like they went to Africa (not Sweden) because they wanted Black slaves, not white slaves. My view is that the War on Drugs is worse than slavery in some ways, and has just replaced slavery. In slavery, suffering could be readily seen in the open fields, in shops, and in other places. To the contrary, mass incarceration keeps unprecedented numbers of young Black men completely out of sight where a lot of the suffering, such as solitary confinement, can't be seen or maybe not even known to many. This appeases the many who don't want to see anyway—out of sight out of mind.

So often the statement is made that our country was founded on an "idea," but crimes against slaves were always behind that idea. The fact is that Blacks by being only 14 percent of the population in the 2000s, is a small group. They're picked on, chased, and less protected by law enforcement, like when a big student might bully a smaller one on the school yard. Likewise, my loved one Sherman was picked on, harassed, chased and stalked by law enforcement when he turned a certain age, and stopped by a police who called about 12 other squad cars for backup—simply harassment and waste of our taxes.

The *Webster's New World Dictionary* defines an idea as the appearance of a thing. It's not the real thing. It hasn't taken form or become real. That's what the struggle has been since slavery to keep Blacks unequal but still appear to be striving. My loved one and countless other young Blacks are routinely arrested and convicted of crimes while whites are largely ignored for the same crimes, especially possession of illegal drugs.

The forces that support that are sanctioned and well-funded by both our government through laws and policies and by individuals. They continue to keep the original idea from taking form. That racism is at the root of the criminal justice system in the 2000s, my time. It's especially spun out of control in the War on Drugs. I don't know about the mafia or whoever before the drug war -- filled the jails. Neither do I know about much crime even before that. But I've seen with my own eyes in the 2000s that most of the drug crime is falsely attributed to young Blacks. According to Marable, "Blacks comprise over 25 percent of all Americans arrested in a given year." (113)

My loved one pleaded guilty for illegal drug possession, but still wasted many, many months of his life in prison. The judge said Sherman's life had many positives, unlike others who appeared before him. The pressure was greatly increased to plead guilty in the War on Drugs. Alexander writes that "when [the war gained full steam in the mid-1980s, the Reagan era] prison admissions for African American's nearly quadrupled in 3 years." (2010, 2012, 98)

For that reason, the way I see it, is President Reagan was worse than any other president for Black's in my lifetime. In hind sight, I feel betrayed and tricked at how he got all that defense increase from everyone's taxes, including mine. Then he switched and used a lot of that defense build-up to take away the freedom of all those thousands of young Black's (my people) and lock them up.

Instead of saving the money to go against possible foreign invaders, the president got permission to use a lot of the build-up money against Blacks. We were not foreign invaders. Blacks did not have atomic bombs either. Military equipment was transferred to law enforcement. They prioritized arrests for illegal drugs, all while targeting young Blacks in unprecedented numbers.

Other presidents followed and continued moving to provide military equipment, intelligence and financial aid to local police departments for drug interdiction, still all while especially targeting young Black men.

Moving on with clarity, a pawn is a chessman of the lowest value. In the dictionary, it is defined as any insignificant person used at another's will or used to advance another's purpose. Thereby, my reasoning is that both Republican and Democratic presidential contenders in the past, have used Blacks as pawns to advance a certain purpose.

For example, as already mentioned, President Reagan's administration quadrupled the number of Black's in prison in three years, to show he could be tough on crime and satisfy those who elected him. Law and order in his administration meant that Blacks in unprecedented numbers were breaking the law.

My opinion is that in like manner, President Clinton followed and created more crime—the three strikes and you're out law. According to (Alexander, 2010, 2012, 56), that law brought into being "dozens of new federal capital crimes…. (the law) resulted in the largest increases in federal and state prison inmates of any president in American history"

That leaves me to conclude that our government under both Republican and Democratic administrations, created crimes that took away the freedom of racial minorities, especially Blacks and imprisoned them in the criminal justice system. That was just as was done in slavery, Slaves were running away. Blacks have always been targeted.

Ms. Alexander reported that "prosecutors admit that they routinely charge people with crimes…they seriously doubt they could ever win in a court," (Alexander, 2020, 110). The pressure is to plead guilty which keeps the prison population up. I believe with all his positives and a jury of his peers, the outcome may have been different for my loved one for a first conviction.

Research notes that "sentencing for minor drug crimes…[in the U.S.] is higher than many countries impose on convicted murderers." (Alexander, 2010, 2012, 89) That's one area where I see our country's exceptionalism has adversely affected my family's life and the lives of many other black families.

Alexander notes that a life sentence for a first-time drug offense is unheard of in the rest of the developed world. Even for high-end drug crimes, it's mostly months for punishment, such as (six months in England), (2010, 2012, 90). I was a living witness to so many young Black men being targeted in the Reagan Era. The bottom line is that mandatory minimum sentencing established under his administration helped keep the prison population up. Arrestees will convict themselves to maybe get a sentence below the mandatory minimum.

My loved one didn't commit one of the most serious crimes as described in the *World Book Encyclopedia* and yet, I felt that his punishment was severe with all the time in solitary confinement. To me, solitary confinement is worse than being in chains as slaves in the fields. Out there, they at least have fresh air and sunshine. Torture was banned in the U.S. in 1948 but is still used because solitary confinement for more than 15 days is considered torture, according to Juan Mendez. Juan Mendez, "Solitary Confinement is Torture," Psychology Today, May 10, 2018.

I think the "get tough on crime" and "law and order" slogans have just meant find some reason to put young Blacks behind bars. I challenge anyone to go to the jails and prisons and see who got locked up.

According to the *World Book Encyclopedia*, a crime is an act of misconduct forbidden by law. Crimes are acts that most people consider evil, acts that lawmakers decide should be regulated in the interest of the community, and so on. In slavery, slaves running away, according to the *World Book Encyclopedia*, would be both committing misconduct and evil—in other words, committing a crime. What kidnapped person even today wouldn't try to run away from a horrible situation such as slavery if he or she got the chance?

The *World Book Encyclopedia* continues that the most serious crimes (kidnapping, rape, murder, burglary, and so on) involve the most severe punishment.

I really believe that both government and law enforcement decided that the drug war was another way to continue many of the wrongs of slavery, especially denying young Blacks freedom and the pursuit of happiness as already mentioned. Add to that "the forces of Jim Crow that especially sought to prevent black people from achieving," (Alexander, 2010, 2012, 213) is being brought back. Achieving is hard to do if you're in jail like so many young Blacks.

Just think back at some of the past acts that were seen as misconduct and illegal down through the ages. Perhaps someone's whim evolved into a law that affected Blacks. The first was running away from the massas, which was called "a criminal nature"; drinking from the wrong fountain was an offense; teaching slaves to read was against the law; sitting down to eat at the lunch counter was an offense; Rosa Parks sitting down on the bus was against the law.

In hindsight, it might sound kind of ridiculous. However, it seems as if it's the same saga that's continued since the civil war -- inequality. There are people who seem to have violent tendencies, especially at the talk of equality. There was the KKK. This kind of thing can't be ignored, because all too often as in the past, loss of someone's freedom or life might happen.

Today, racial violence has been incorporated and is funded with everyone's government taxes. What used to be KKK violence can be lumped together with police brutality before arrests, and solitary confinement after lock-up. Since our taxes finance the government, everyone is complicit in supporting that violence, willingly or unwillingly.

My realization is that the lion's share of suffering from this violence in the past has been by especially Blacks, my people. It's still disproportionately experienced due to the War on Drugs and the criminal justice system by unprecedented numbers of people of color, especially Blacks.

But attitudes of some may still linger against Blacks that "slaves ran away." There maybe some, still brooding over that loss. My loved one is made a target for drug offenses today, as if he and countless other Blacks inherited a criminal nature that was somehow passed down from whatever slave ran away.

I've heard whites ask why they should be blamed and asked to help pay for reparations when they were not living back then. By the same reasoning, my family wasn't living back then either.

Locking inmates in cells after police arrests, is followed with months and sometimes years of solitary confinement at the whim of prison guards and officers. Being in prison can cause alarming "overall health affects," according to (Pfaff, 120). Fresh air and sunlight, which was plentiful for captured slaves in the fields, is denied in prison for many. Those provisions that God made free to all people, a Harvard Health Special Report says, "are critical for good health," *Harvard Health Publications, Vitamins and Minerals,* 2006,16) It seems like some criminal justice system leaders want to remake the world that our loving God made in their own evil image by building prisons. According to *World Book Encyclopedia,* 1973, people in ancient and medieval time rarely used imprisonment as a penalty. Pfaff states that "in the United States, many feel that one of the goals of prison is for the prisoner to suffer" (120). Most other western countries don't view prison that way.

Unlike most any other war, this War on Drugs is not to protect U.S. citizens. My opinion is that its main mission is for unjust, biased punishment of U.S. citizens of color (especially Blacks). That's what is happening. You can visit jails and prisons and see for yourselves who is behind bars. What's noble about using the full power of the government on its own citizens? Where's the nobleness and greatness in this war? To repeat, the government stacked the deck to win. How can a poorer, disadvantaged family in the wealth gap in these United States defend against airplanes, big tanks, surveillance, and other methods? The government designed the unlevel playing field and compels black and brown people especially to wrestle against all that. It's so controversial that many states have already decriminalized marijuana in the War on Drugs. Many, however, still keep it illegal, like the union did when some states wanted to keep slavery and some did not.

I'm reminded of a story I heard from a Black doctor on some TV station. He said if you see a fish floating on the pond, you think maybe something is wrong with that one fish. Maybe it choked on something. If you see a pond full of fish floating, you look for something in the pond. Likewise, if you see a few young Black men in prison corresponding to 14 percent of the total Black U.S. population, you think they could have committed a crime. When you see unprecedented wall-to-wall cells of young Black men and very few young whites or other races, there's something in the pond—racism in the criminal justice system.

If a U.S. president ever committed to get tough on racism, like "get tough on crime," then who would fill the cells?

I repeat, as is so often stated, our country was founded on an "idea." A fact is that Blacks, being only 14 percent of the population, are a small group, picked on, chased, less protected by law enforcement, and outrageously hated by many akin to Hitler.

To repeat, the dictionary defines an idea as not the real thing. It hasn't taken form or become real. The struggle since slavery has been to keep Blacks as unequal. These forces are many and are still sanctioned by both our government through laws and policies and individuals. They continue to keep the original idea from taking form, and remain an appearance only.

MY VIEW OF THE CRIMINAL JUSTICE SYSTEM

BEFORE SHERMAN WAS ARRESTED, I KNEW VERY LITTLE ABOUT criminal justice. As already mentioned, the only criminal justice TV show that ever interested me was *Perry Mason*. It was entertaining. However, back then in the late 1950s, living in the South, I cannot remember ever seeing a young Black male defendant in any of those shows. The criminal justice system as it is today in 2022 with so many young Black men's lives being ruined, is not entertaining to me. I don't get pleasure at seeing someone being mistreated and harmed, especially my own people. If all that had been shown on *Perry Mason*, it would not have interested me.

To say the least, I was very upset, disheartened, and disgusted at Sherman's arrest and even more so in the false, unjust, racist War on Drugs. I say unjust because law enforcement selectively ignores large numbers of whites, but with bias, selects large numbers of Blacks, captures them, and locks them up because they can. So many whites (but not all) who have evil hearts and spirits want this. In most wars, there's been recruitment and volunteers of both whites and blacks and others.

I try to keep up with what's going on in the world. Criminal justice TV shows have changed from a few, mostly white adult men on *Perry Mason* in the 1950s being locked up, to showing an unprecedented number of young Black men imprisoned in the 2000s, all because of the drug war. I'm very concerned to see on the news how so many young Black males with promise who could have been my students are brutalized and shot by law enforcement. On the *Perry Mason* show, I don't remember seeing such brutality against young or older whites who were shot in the back sixty times before being taken into custody.

No one in my family thinks Sherman deserved to be locked up due to the War on Drugs. It's an evil program that created crimes, just like slavery's wrongs. I'm sure many other Black families feel the same about their loved ones. We do love our families too. I have met other Blacks who were caught as dumbfounded as me, at the criminalizing atrocity of a loved one jailed for a non-violent marijuana drug offense.

It may not be well known and so I repeat Alexander's claim that, "since the days of slavery, Black men have been depicted and understood as criminals," (2020, 298). That understanding of a ("criminal nature") has unfortunately stayed in the minds of slave-holders and some of their offspring down through the centuries. It began as slaves who had been stolen, tried running away from the master, which was called a crime. Police were appointed to catch the runaway slaves. Their descendants are now called villains. In my opinion, the real villains were the kidnappers who were not captured and punished for their theft crimes.

Of the many young men in the family who I love, Sherman is the only one who had to do time. This all happened because of, as research reports, an increase in biased law enforcement practices in the War on Drugs. According to Alexander (2010, 2012) young Black men are several times more likely to be arrested and sent to federal prison than Whites (see page 11, Alexander for these several multiple cites (2010, 2012) 1st paragraph). That's just biased treatment by any stretch of the imagination. Why?

My opinion is it's conscious, willful, bad judgement

that this attitude continues today. Slaves ran away, and their descendants inherited that alleged, trumped up phony "criminal nature" in the War on Drugs centuries later. They are now still deemed bad in the 2000s. The drug war is the program that has replaced slavery and serves to continue to justify the excuse that Blacks inherited a "criminal nature."

According to Alexander, "More black men are imprisoned today than at any other moment in our nation's history" (2010, 2012, 180). That's all due to the War on Drugs. I repeat that that replaced slavery and continues many of its wrongs. Tyra Banks stated that "hundreds of thousands of black men…did not walk out on their families voluntarily; they were taken away in handcuffs…[due to] the War on Drugs," (180). That was the case with my loved one and countless others' young black loved ones.

Alexander also writes that "a social psychologist…found that black fathers not living at home are more likely to keep in contact with their children than fathers of any other ethnic or racial group," (Alexander, 2010, 2012, 179).

Frederick Douglass, who devoted his life to the fight for Negroes in the 1800s, said that "Blacks are condemned for no other reason than the color of their skin," (Alexander 2010, 2011, 140). Now in the 2000s, it's worse, with all the tanks, helicopters, surveillance, and other tactics. As already mentioned, being a young Black man, according to Michelle Alexander's report, means Blacks are many, many times more likely to be arrested in general than whites and sent to federal prison. It's up to eighty to ninety times more likely in some states on drug charges. That's just a preposterous, blatantly racist policy. Alexander reports, and I agree, that many, many Black men are in prison for the same crimes that go largely ignored in middle and upper-class white communities, namely "possession and sale of illegal drugs," (2010, 2012, 172). I saw for myself who was locked up.

At Sherman's guilty plea, there was no conviction for a

violent charge. His offense was classified as a non-violent illegal drug sale. Drug sales are mostly consensual anyway, not usually involving 911 calls. Alexander further states that "African Americans are not significantly more likely to use or sell prohibited drugs than whites, but they are made criminals at drastically higher rates for the same conduct as whites," (2010, 2012, 197). My view is that white privilege keeps many whites out of prison; that's an option my loved one and millions of other Blacks didn't have. They were locked up.

Research further notes that the criminal justice system has always been racist, (Alexander, 2010, 2012, 187). I agree. In the late 1950s, I didn't know anyone locked up when I was in high school. Racism still mostly benefits the majority of Whites, at the expense of Blacks and others. The courts are highly prejudiced. I've witnessed that with my own eyes and ears too, supporting Sherman at various court appearances. Sherman faced white judges, biased white prosecutors, and other mostly biased white court administrators. They determined he was guilty. Then he faced the same white faces who determined punishment. There's no difference now than from when slaves were owned by slave owners who were in charge of justice.

While supporting Sherman, I never saw a white defendant waiting in the hearing room. When I visited Sherman in prison, I didn't see a white inmate locked up. Alexander goes on to report that "racist bias in the drug war is a major reason that one in every 14 Black men was behind bars in 2006, compared to 1 in 106 white men," (Alexander, 2010, 2011, 100).

In the American criminal justice system, the law is white and was made by mostly white legislators. They made the laws and policies and established courts mostly of their own construction. They stacked the deck to win. Alexander writes, and as it seems to be the case to me also, that those in power are trying to label young Black men as felons by age twenty-one (Alexander, 2010, 2012, 192). From what I saw while supporting Sherman at hearings, they're doing it mostly with non-violent drug charges and charges for non-violent behavior. Many young black men labeled felons are behind bars for non-violent behavior. Just as the slave label did, the felon label also keeps many many Blacks from rising, as slaves couldn't rise out of slavery, their masters had to free them.

According to Alexander, (2010, 2012, 99) white youth have about "three times the number of drug-related emergency room visits as their African American counter parts." She also reports that "the most of those arrested for drug crimes are not charged with serious offenses," (2010, 2012, 209). She adds that [Most people] in state prison on drug charges have no history of violence or significant selling activity" (209). Research notes that the "war on drugs" has been waged primarily against non-violent low-level offenders in poor communities of color (209). Law enforcement is giving many of our Black children a felony conviction like my loved one, overwhelmingly for non-violent crime.

The *World Book Encyclopedia* defines a felony as a crime where imprisonment is for more than a year or death (i.e., murder, robbery, burglary, kidnapping, treason). A lesser violation is a misdemeanor, but with the War on Drugs, the legislators made changes. Selling illegal drugs used to be a lesser violation than the crimes just listed. However, to suit their own sinister purpose to (punish Black and Brown people and lock them up), they made that crime (possession and sale of illegal drugs) non-violent at first. It then evolved into a felony to require prison time because a misdemeanor didn't necessarily require a prison stay. Alexander states, "Because Blacks were disproportionately charged with felonies—in fact—some crimes, were specifically defined as felonies...to suppress the Black vote," (2010, 2012, 192).

It seems that they changed their own laws, making, possessing, and selling illegal drugs a felony to target young Blacks to make them guilty of a crime that would require time behind bars. "Until 1988, one year of imprisonment had been the maximum for possession of any amount of any drug," (Alexander, 2010, 2012, 54). In my opinion, judges, prosecutors, police, and others just wanted to make more money. Research notes that violent crime was declining (there were not as many murders and similar crimes) in my opinion they made misdemeanors (possessing and selling drugs) felonies to raise their own pay.

It is reported that they started locking up excessively high numbers for nonviolent drug offenses. The rules were redesigned and they rounded up Afro-Americans for minor, small-time, less serious offenses through sweeps, suspicious stops, and searches. Research says that many of the small-time offenders would not have gone to prison in the past, (Pfaff, 59). Instead of getting a second job, as many lower income people do when work slows down, criminal justice employees made things a felony that used to be misdemeanors to put more people behind bars, so they would be paid more. It may have seemed to the public like more serious crimes than misdemeanors were being committed.

In Sherman's case, when I was told that the FBI was coming to my home, my mind went to Brianna Taylor. Those five white agents certainly were not welcome at my house.

The FBI is ruthless in breaking into people's houses, and may have broken into mine pursuing someone for a non-violent drug offense. All that money was taken out of my taxes to handcuff someone who is non-violent and not a threat, namely, my loved one. The FBI has no regard or respect for my home or the things of Christ. It made me sick to my stomach to think back to Brianna Taylor, wondering if they would repeat that behavior at my home for my family to have to deal with.

When they knocked on my door, and then entered my home, I shouted -- "Ronald Reagan told you all to stop investigating as many whites like yourselves who were mostly older and richer. That's why you are here to pick up my loved one who is Black, young, and doesn't have a white-collar job."

In essence, they shifted the focus from the more affluent,

older white criminals to the poorer and younger Blacks because President Reagan's administration directed them to do that. That's the same as in colonial times, with slavery, when the government sent slave-traders to Africa, a poorer continent with people of color, not to Sweden to get slaves.

One of the five agents seemed chatty; perhaps, his conscience pricked a bit. He seemed to want to justify his presence at my home. He asked, "Don't you think people who commit violent crime should go to jail?"

I said, "Yes, but my loved one hasn't killed anybody or raped anyone or shot up any merchant's business. What's his violent offense?"

Alexander's report on Black crime shows that Sherman, as already mentioned, was one of many who was rounded up [and went] to prison for engaging in...the same crimes that go largely ignored in middle - and upper - class white communities"—possession and sale of illegal drugs" (2010, 2012, 172).

I can remember before the 1980s how many officers in the penal system weren't going to drive their cars that much on some of those washboard dirt roads. You can probably remember those roads too. That changed for whatever reason.

I think it was the War on Drugs that brought about consequential change in the penal system after 1980, with the change directed especially at young Blacks. One change with the drug war was that felony no longer meant mostly murder, robbery, burglary, kidnapping, treason, and similar crimes.

As already mentioned, in my opinion, it seems that when the War on Drugs was advanced, the rules were then rigged and redesigned, and countless African-American men were rounded up for minor, small-time, less serious offenses through sweeps, suspicious stops, and searches. Officers started driving down those washboard dirt roads, maybe more of them being paved now. It's reported that many of these small-time offenders would not have gone to prison in the past, (Pfaff, 59). Instead of getting a second job as many lower income people do when work slows down, criminal justice employees made non-violent drug offenses felonies that used to be misdemeanors, in my opinion, so they would be paid more. As already mentioned, violent crimes were declining.

They use twisted talk so maybe no one will notice. Sherman said later, "They just want bodies." From what I experienced and saw, it's an unprecedented number of young bodies of color (especially Blacks) in jail. According to Alexander, (2010, 2011) "thousands of people have had years of their lives wasted in prison—years they would have been free if they had been white," (2010, 2011,114).

I heard stated on television something similar to-the FBI was formed for violent offenses. My wonder is then, why such a role in the drug war? Most of the marijuana drug offenses are classified as non-violent. It's just validation that they change the laws' wording to suit their convenient purpose.

Since there's a preponderant amount of young Blacks being convicted and imprisoned for non-violent offenses-Who does law enforcement (the FBI) need to protect from physical harm if it's mostly non-violent behavior, and why? Are all those expansions of jails and prisons for non-violent people? Legislators should revisit that non-violent nomenclature, and maybe on the merits change something. The laws and policies of non-violence are totally contradictory to the premise that all those young Blacks need to be taken off the streets to keep streets safe. They then say out of the other sides of their mouths, that their offenses are non-violent. When I hear, *violent*, I think of physical injury, but not non-violent. If there's no injury -- Who is all the punishment behind bars protecting?

In Sherman's first hearing that I attended, the prejudiced white judge accused Sherman of violating a rule and posting on his Instagram. Sherman said he didn't post but the judge said she believed he did. If he didn't do it himself, she said that she believed he told someone else to. I was flabbergasted to know what all those billions of dollars in the criminal justice system's budget was paying for. With no evidence, this judge's personal biased opinions allowed her to issue a warrant. I saw the "spiritual wickedness" mentioned in Ephesians 6:12 in these high places, where people decided if the defendant would be free or locked up. That's who Sherman was challenged to wrestle against; some wicked thinkers (but not all are) prejudging him by negative stereotypes. They've probably seen these people on television or at the movies or wherever. The scripture goes on to say my young loved one was challenged to "wrestle against these rulers of darkness and principalities" (that's the whole U.S. government). The court document was the United States versus Sherman.

In essence, since the biased judge said Sherman was guilty without giving a shred of evidence, I wondered (well whatever happened to innocent until proven guilty) the mantra I'd heard so often. When the evidence came back proving that Sherman didn't post and someone else posted, I was surprised at how the whites in charge were allowed to steamroll over everything and prevail. The judge did not apologize for her wrong accusation and this is what justice is. My opinion is the judge believed Sherman was guilty (just as Fredrick Douglas said in the 1800s) because of the color of his skin. She could see his skin color.

When the legislators made marijuana criminal, they knew this would entice some people to try it, just like cigarettes (which are also drugs). All along, I believe the intentions were to enforce the marijuana drug laws they would make, primarily against Blacks. That's what happened. They arrested more blacks, sending them to federal prison, as already mentioned, from four times up to eighty to ninety times more often than whites. You can see for yourselves who is behind bars on drug charges.

It seems that the U.S. really adopted John Locke's ideas straight out of the colonial era. Perhaps this judge knew of Locke's advice to a friend "to feel nothing at others' misfortune,"

(Kendi, 59). Perhaps this judge, and maybe many others, internalized Locke's preaching as the gospel. Locke helped draw up the Carolinas Constitution and was knowledgeable about British colonialism and slavery. Perhaps that's why so many whites are indifferent to the large numbers of Blacks incarcerated due to the drug war. Many whites say, "In God we trust." I trust in God too. To me, indifference to someone else's misfortune is some weird Christian grace. I heard that terminology in a sermon on a religious television station, and I agree. One is under some kind of "weird and different grace" if he or she allows all those indifferent feelings toward others' misfortune.

I am disheartened and sad to learn how so many educated Blacks seem to have allowed themselves to be brainwashed into believing the same as many prejudiced whites; that our young Black men are just bad, broke the law, and deserve to be put in prison. Instead of being outraged that a young Black man broke the law, which changes sometimes on whims, without notice, I tell them what they should be outraged about is young Black men, because of the color of their skin—are ten times more likely than whites to be arrested, exponentially on up to eighty to ninety times more likely than whites to be sent to federal prison on drug charges (see page 11, multiple cites from Alexander, (2010, 2012) 1st paragraph).

Those in power will make anything illegal to suit their own whims and purposes, and enforce it on Blacks in large numbers. Ages ago, the government made it illegal to teach slaves to read and now the War on Drugs has locked up unprecedented numbers of Black men. It seems that laws were always made against slaves for something and now they're still being made against descendants of slaves, in unprecedented numbers for illegal drugs.

I feel our young Black men deserve as much opportunity and support to develop their potential as anyone else. As a teacher, I did not see my young Black male students as villains any more than I can believe that slaves were misfits for being trapped and put in chains to maintain slavery.

Some Blacks also say the young men chose to commit crimes and it's their own fault. That's how those in power want Black folk to think. My reasoning is that the War on Drugs, just like slavery, was designed to make a profit off making life miserable for others, especially young Blacks. Young black men had no voice in that, and neither did they have a voice in making the policy where they are more likely to be arrested – exponentially several times more than whites, depending on the state.

Common sense and critical, logical thinking will tell a person that all those Africans who were brought to the U.S. in chains all those years wasn't due to poor choices, and neither was it their own fault that they could have avoided. That's why weapons and chains were used to coerce them. No matter what the African's situation, the British government's and the U.S. government's policies were designed to be clandestine enough to entrap those slaves.

The powers that be, knew that you don't know what you don't know. Therefore, my opinion is that how Blacks are being captured and put in the criminal system, in unprecedented numbers, is left out of the school curriculum intentionally, as a part of the entrapment plan, just like traffic rules. The police try to park in obscure places where it's hard to be spotted. Some political leaders and others don't want you to see, and so injustices, especially on large numbers of Blacks, are left out of the school curriculum as a plan to facilitate their entrapment.

I can't believe any of Sherman's white teachers told him he could be up to eighty or ninety times more likely to be arrested and put in prison than their own white biological children. There are so many more white teachers than black these days. Some white teachers may not have known themselves that their Black male students were ten times or more likely than their white biological child to be arrested, convicted, and locked-up. I didn't know that before writing this book.

In metaphoric terms, I see that what I call modern-day chains, have replaced the iron and steel chains used on slaves. My view is that the modern-day chains are just as strong in helping entrap an overwhelmingly large number of young people of color (especially Blacks) in our nation's prisons to take away their freedom today, as were used to trap slaves.

The modern chains no longer bruise and scar the flesh like the iron and steel ones, but they still can cause irreparable harm and trauma. They can leave scars too. The chains have been changed to fit the circumstances of today's times.

I'm sure many Africans going about their everyday lives didn't know they were about to be captured and lose their freedom. Likewise, most of our young Black males and others have no voice in planning. Therefore, they don't necessarily recognize the elaborate schemes leading them to entrapment and loss of their freedom either.

African slaves didn't know and couldn't avoid the process either. Some of what I call (today's modern chains) are as follows:

1. Police target Blacks. They go into poorer, disadvantaged neighborhoods of color and make sweeps. Going to the hood guarantees they'll get mostly Blacks.
2. Police are rewarded with huge cash grants from our taxes for the number of arrests they make and for making drug enforcement a top priority.
3. One in three young African Americans is currently under the control of the criminal justice system, in prison, in jail, on probation, or on parole.
4. Minor traffic stops are used as an excuse for the police to hunt for drugs, although there is no evidence of any drug law violation. One is always supposed to pull over and stop for the police.

5. In consenting to the search, the young driver may not believe and may not be told by police that he or she is free to remain silent or refuse to answer questions. As long as you give consent, the police have the authority to stop, interrogate, and search you for any reason or for no reason at all.

6. The worst schools are in Black neighborhoods and often lack resources.

7. Many more Blacks are suspended from school than whites and other races especially in schools with the zero tolerance policy. Both students are suspended, no matter which one started the disturbance.

8. The zero tolerance program in schools was designed to help feed the prison-complex with a steady supply of inmates who would already be used to being warehoused.

9. This country is consumed with racist ideas.

10. The rules were rigged, changed, and designed to round up exceedingly high numbers for minor, small-time, less serious offenses and nonviolent drug offenses through sweeps, suspicious stops, and searches. Many of the small-time offenders would not have gone to prison in the past, (Pfaff, 59).

11. No other country in the world imprisons so many of its racial ethnic minorities. The U.S. imprisons a larger percentage of its Black population than South Africa in the height of apartheid. The U.S. rate of incarceration has indeed soared, but stayed stable or declined in other industrialized nations.

12. The U.S. crime rate dipped below the international norm, but is still six or ten times greater than other industrialized nations, mostly due to the drug war.

13. Almost half of all prisoners in the U.S. at any given time are Black (Marable, 112).

14. Racist policies and laws are from racist ideas.

15. "More Black men are imprisoned today than at any other moment in our nation's history" (Alexander, 2010, 2012, 180).
16. Mass incarceration of people of color is a big part of the reason that a black child born today is less likely to be raised by both parents than a black child born during slavery (Alexander, 2010, 2012, 180).

THE TRIAL

THE HIGHEST AND FINAL DECISION MAKER AT SHERMAN'S SENTENCING was the judge who weighed all the evidence—much like Pilate prosecuted Jesus in the Bible and said he found no fault in him. With my loved one, I am reminded of how the Hebrews, Jews, descendants of Abraham were in the minority in the Roman court, as Sherman was in the U.S. court.

Like I said in the Preface, the Bible is my compass for living; it is where I get my direction and the courage to be.

In Luke 18:2, God said, "There was in a city, a judge, which feared not God, neither regarded man." This covers a lot of judges like Sherman's judge and could apply to any judge. At his sentencing, the White judge told the court that Sherman was unlike many who appear before him.

1. He came from a supportive family.
2. He grew up attending church.
3. The judge said he received many good character letters for Sherman.
4. He had no criminal record.
5. He didn't drop out of school.
6. He had some community college.
7. This was his first conviction on an illegal drug charge.

8. He had a legal permit to carry the gun he had, but he hadn't shot anyone with it.
9. He expressed regret and said he would not do this again, that the judge said he sensed was sincere.

When I was growing up, I used to think people in jail were bad and maybe had killed or assaulted or robbed someone. I knew these things were illegal. They were against human law, but also were warned about in the Ten Commandments, God's law. But illegal seemingly changed or evolved and justice evolved. My eyes were opened when I was arrested and put in jail along with others in the lunch counter sit-ins for trying to sit down and eat. I had never thought of myself as a criminal, but somehow I was bad for doing that. Dr. Martin Luther King's work, to me, determined that the U.S. laws were not necessarily laws from our Supreme God. Unlike those who wrote the Constitution, leaders making laws these days don't necessarily talk of consulting God in their thinking. Dr. King said, some laws and policies were unjust themselves in the first place. They were just bad laws. For most of those charged in the sit-ins, the charges were dropped.

Likewise, I don't feel like Sherman is a bad person for being arrested for marijuana. I don't feel that his possession and sale of marijuana was any more of a threat to society than my dad having a carton of Camel cigarettes or my sitting at the lunch counter. Like Pilate in the Bible, the judge could have said that he found little fault in Sherman. My dad smoked two packs of Camel cigarettes a day, raised a family, and was a deacon in the church for about thirty years. Alexander reports "that marijuana is less harmful than tobacco," (2010, 2011, 60). Cigarettes contain the drug nicotine. I don't see where someone selling marijuana up the street threatens my community any more than my dad's Camels were a threat.

During Sherman's trial, since the judge acknowledged that Sherman's life was unlike those who usually appeared before him, I wondered what would be different in the verdict. Like Pilate, this judge found a lot of good, positive factors in Sherman. However, with the judge (Pharoah), Sherman's positive factors didn't matter. It seems that Jesus's prosecutor, a Roman, didn't show prejudice toward Jesus. I think the only thing that mattered to the judge, was Sherman was Black.

The judge stayed true to the nature of Pharoah. Even though he touted, as already mentioned, Sherman's life was different -- it wasn't good enough because it wasn't perfect, as Jesus and the judge's probably wasn't either. The judge had made it clear in the first hearing with us that he received advisory guidelines but wasn't bound to follow those legislative guidelines. He could use his own discretion and he did not divulge those advisory guidelines that he received.

In spite of all the evidence and a lot of positives, I cannot say that God hardened the judge's heart. I believe he hardened his own heart. With his own biased discretion, he added many more months at Sherman's sentencing hearing. The advisory guidelines could have recommended dismissal with time served or community service or probation, especially with all the positives. Instead, the judge chose to make Sherman a felon, though he said Sherman's life was different with many positives. How do you get a felon out of a mostly positive life? In my opinion, the jails and prisons didn't get that full with unprecedented numbers of young Black men, if some were being convicted with non-violent behavior, which used to be less than a felony. They are making our young Black men felons. As Alexander states, "arrests that result in prison sentences (rather than dismissals, community service or probation) have quadrupled," (2020, 77). My wonder is how many dismissals, community service or probation sentences this judge had given, if any, and to whom.

I don't know what level felony the judge gave Sherman, but according to (Pfaff, 70) "prosecutors determine who gets sent to prison and for how long." Pfaff goes on to note that "prosecutors can restrict judges to narrow sentence ranges" (131), but judges can sentence more on their own. Pfaff continues that prosecutors can be lenient or practice upcharging (73). Alexander notes that some judges "impose sentences for drug crimes that are often longer than those convicted murderers receive" (2010, 2011, 89).

Studies show that "among youth who have never been sent to a juvenile prison before, [Blacks face the harshest discrimination] African Americans were more than six times as likely as whites to be sentenced to prison for *identical crimes*" (Alexander, 2010, 2012, 118). That kind of prosecutor discretion is allowed; it's "racial biases infecting decision making," (118), especially toward Blacks. Many prosecutors desire to keep the status quo (mass incarceration) like many wanted to keep slavery.

Prosecutors know that there's no "meaningful check…of their discretion in charging" (Alexander, 2010, 2012, 117) unless they make explicit racist remarks. They also know that their conscious and unconscious biases are allowed to flourish. Alexander writes that "Whites are far more successful than African Americans and Latinos in the plea bargaining process; in fact, [at virtually every stage of pretrial negotiation, whites are more successful than non whites]" (117).

My opinion and critical thinking is that many prosecutors have some of the same outrageous biases as the masses of whites regarding the unprecedented number of Blacks they charge. My further analysis is that it's like driving. If some drivers don't see the cops chasing them when they're speeding and could get a traffic ticket, they might not think about checking themselves. Likewise, knowing that there is no meaningful check on their prosecutor discretion; it's like a driver who has the discretion to speed or not. In like manner, the prosecutor has discretion to bring charges or not -- because no one is watching.

In my further reasoning, that's why there are unprecedented

numbers of Blacks in prison today. Prosecutors have their minds focused on getting to their destination (as in driving), which is keeping the prisons full. That enables them to keep their jobs and continue to maintain their high standards of living. They target Blacks.

Most school curriculums do not cover teaching these legislated injustices, although a mission of schools is to prepare students for future reality. For blacks, that is to know more than the reading and math. They need to know (Marable, 112) as already mentioned, he notes that almost half of all prisoners in the U.S. at any given time are black. Schools are not preparing young blacks to handle the possible imprisonment that unprecedented large numbers of them could face if trends continue.

Concerning prosecutors, between 1994 and 2008, the number of felony cases...rose by almost 40 percent (Pfaff, 72). Pfaff noted that the chance that an arrest would lead to a felony case grew from about one in three to two in three. Since it's the prosecutors who decide whether to file felony charges (Pfaff, 70); My opinion is they made more felonies because they could. As stated in (Micah 2:1), it was "in the power of their hand." There was a "drop in the number of arrests during this time," (Pfaff, 72).

Blacks are four to ten times and on up more likely than whites to be convicted and imprisoned on drug offenses. The reason for that is that blacks are targeted and made felons at much higher rates than whites. It's the same old scheme that was in colonial America. It is an attempt in the 2000s to keep blacks at the lowest level of society as was done to preserve slavery. Now, that's being achieved by the criminal justice system to preserve the War on Drugs. Instead of using chains and weapons, as was done to preserve slavery, the criminal justice system is well-funded to preserve the War on Drugs that has replaced slavery. They use guns and handcuffs now in the 2000s.

My view is that, in the criminal justice system, they just

started charging less serious crime the same as murder (a felony) first to keep the prison population up. They changed misdemeanors to felonies to have more bodies locked up. Second, to repeat, "Blacks were disproportionately charged with felonies, in fact, some crimes were specifically defined as felonies" (Alexander, 2010, 2012, 192) to prevent Blacks from voting. That's corrupt, racist legislated prosecutor discretion. Even after release, the law requires penalties from states to ban individuals with a drug related felony from employment.

Continuing with Sherman's trial (through my own lens), the judge's actions showed he held a personal negative, prejudiced attitude about Blacks, just as the masses of whites (but not all). To repeat, research reports that even though many don't believe they have biases, studies prove that, when tested, police have relatively high levels of bias.

Alexander reports that TV stories and other media including political rhetoric have disproportionately featured African Americans associated with street crime over the past three decades, (2020, 133). She continues that many studies found that "much racial bias...operates unconsciously and automatically – even among law enforcement officials, genuinely committed to equal treatment under the law," (135).

Nearing the end of Sherman's sentencing hearing, the judge actually said his concern was how he would look if he gave Sherman "a slap on the wrist." That's exactly what many whites get and I feel that this judge wouldn't have any special concern with his white peers seeing him give a young white man a "slap on the wrist." I processed that statement as the judge's (paramount) concern, was how he would look, not real justice on the merits of all the evidence for Sherman, which should have been his greatest concern.

The judge further stated that he did not want to set precedent. In spite of all those positive factors that the judge was touting, he suddenly switched to hostility. He had said to the court more than once that Sherman's life was unlike those who appeared before him. However, beginning his conclusion, the judge veered hostilely to not wanting to set precedent and change anything.

I, an eighty year-old Black grandparent, have analyzed racist experiences and subtle racist rhetoric all my life. I processed the judge's statement that he did "not want to set precedent" through my own lens, like this. It was his discriminatory racist thinking and his judge's discretion that no matter how many positive factors, this first conviction for a nonviolent drug charge made Sherman an instant villain, a felon, because he is Black. To the contrary, according to Alexander, "white drug offenders are rarely arrested…they are consistently more likely to avoid prison and felony charges even when they are repeat offenders…black offenders, by contrast, are routinely labeled felons," (2010, 2012, 189). It wasn't an option for Sherman and unprecedented numbers of other young Blacks to avoid prison and felony charges. That's routine. The judge just saw a Black male stereotype consciously and unconsciously in Sherman. I believe he had already made up his mind because of that.

Too many young Black men have experienced, and can make the statement made by a forty three year old African American experiencing scorn and contempt. He said he'd never been homeless until he left the penitentiary…."We [Black men] have three strikes against us: 1) because we are black 2) because we are a Black male, and the final strike is a felony," (Alexander, 2010, 2012, 163). Frederick Douglas spoke of the "cruel hand" resurging over 150 years ago, and has appeared again.

I repeat that, too many young Black men have experienced, and can make the statement made by a forty-three year old African American experiencing scorn and contempt. He said he'd never been homeless until he left the penitentiary…"We [black men] have three strikes against us: 1) because we are black, and 2) because we are a black male and the final strike is a felony," (Alexander, 2010, 2012, 163). Frederick Douglass spoke of the "cruel hand" resurging over 150 years ago, and has appeared again.

Sherman's judge was that judge in Luke 18:2: "He feared not God, neither regarded man." He did not regard Sherman as a child of God, and neither did he regard (the people who wrote all the good character letters) that were suggested that attested to Sherman's good lifestyle. The judge's lips touted positives from the evidence, but his actions said this is a villain, a felon because of the color of his skin.

Not wanting to set precedent, in my opinion, also meant, not wanting to change the following facts that he surely knew.

1.) "Blacks were disproportionally charged with felonies, in fact some crimes were specifically defined as felonies" to prevent Blacks from voting, (Alexander, 2010, 2012, 192).

2.) [Thousands] of Black men are in prison for the same drug crimes that go largely ignored...in white communities (Alexander, 2020, 214).

3.) Whites are consistently more likely to avoid prison and felony charges, even if they are repeat offenders.

4.) More African American adults are under correctional custody today than were enslaved in 1850, a decade before the Civil War.

5.) You can't be gainfully employed and become successful in prison. The judge wanted to continue harshly punishing Blacks with additional time, like he did Sherman. He gave him many more months, at his own discretion.

6.) Although the judge said more than once that Sherman's life was different than many who came before him, the judge's action did not show a difference in the verdict (it was not dismissal or community service or probation) because Sherman is still Black.

7.) More Black men are imprisoned today in the U.S. than at any other moment in our nation's history. The judge did not want to change that. What has made today better if more Blacks are imprisoned now than at any time in the past?

8.) It's fiction that most illegal drug use sales happen in the ghetto. It happens everywhere. But Black men have been admitted to state prison for this at a rate thirteen times higher than white men (Alexander, 2010, 2012, 100). Sherman's judge didn't want to change any of that.

9.) People of color (especially Blacks) are convicted of drug offenses at rates out of all proportion of other drug crime.

10.) One in three young African American men is currently under the control of the criminal justice system in prison, in jail, on probation, or on parole. The judge didn't want to change that.

11.) According to Alexander, they want to brand young Black men as felons—as many as they can by age twenty-one (Alexander, 2010, 2012, 192). The judge didn't want to change that.

12.) Mandatory minimum sentencing was imposed in the Reagan era that replaced the one-year imprisonment that had been the maximum until 1988. It applies also to people with no prison or prior criminal conviction (Alexander, 2010, 2012, 53). The judge didn't want to change that.

13.) In the House's hearing in the summer of 2022, it was reported that young Black men are four times more likely to be convicted and imprisoned for marijuana. Alexander reported that young Black men are ten times more likely to be arrested in general, thirteen times (Alexander 2010, 2012, 100) more likely to be admitted to federal prison on drug charges, and up to eighty to ninety times more likely in seven states (189). The judge didn't want to change any of that.

14.) "Mass incarceration of people of color is a big reason that a Black child today is less likely to be raised by both parents than a Black child born in slavery" (Alexander, 2010, 2011, 180). The judge didn't want to change that.

15.) One in three young Afro-American men will serve time in prison if current trends continue (Alexander, 2010, 2012, 9). The judge didn't want to change that.

16.) It is estimated that three out of four young Black men (and nearly all those in the poorest neighborhoods) can expect to serve time in prison (Alexander, 2020, 8). The judge didn't want to change that.

17.) It's an unlevel playing field with police going to poor communities of color (especially Black) to round up non-Whites.

18.) Many good-hearted white people are generous to others and even kind to some Black people, but don't believe it's the right time yet for equality.

Moving on, the judge knew that all sorts of hideous things could happen in federal prison. At the prosecution of Jesus, Pilate said, "I find no fault in this man." With all those positive factors the judge touted for Sherman, as in the prosecution of Jesus the judge could have said he found little fault in Sherman. He said Sherman's life was unlike those who appear before him.

Instead, this judge wanted this young Black man to experience the worst. To me, his discretion was akin to Hitler's. He knew Sherman would probably have to go to solitary confinement, which according to a special report from the American Medical Association (AMA), could cause health damage and, in some cases, death, Martha Waggoner, "Lawsuit Challenges State's use of solitary confinement", U.S. News, Oct. 16, 2019.

The judge knew that whites are less likely to be subjected

to solitary confinement even (as already mentioned) with multiple convictions. That's blatant unequal treatment under the law, akin to Hitler's thinking. The judge said one thing and did another. He touted Sherman's positives; that he was unlike those who appeared before him, but he ruled as if Sherman had many negatives instead of positives.

To repeat, solitary confinement can cause adverse and unfortunate health damages, as the AMA notes, and as reported by Waggoner. The judge should have known that but didn't want to change it, not even for a young Black male he touted as having a mostly positive lifestyle throughout his life. The judge should have known that policy makers say solitary confinement is overused and can do more harm than good.

This torture is what both our Democratic and Republican brother and sister Evangelicans are supporting. As in Ephesians 6:12 Sherman, my babe in Christ and countless others' Black and Brown loved ones are compelled to wrestle against all this spiritual wickedness in these high criminal justice system positions.

I found that torture was banned in the U.S. in 1948 under the Universal Declaration of Human Rights. My wonder is why our leaders are still making all citizens fund it with our taxes through the criminal justice system. It just seems like something that those who embrace the Hitler mindset would do.

According to Mendez, a U.N. special reporter on torture, any period of isolation longer than fifteen days should be considered abusive, (Mendez). All our tax dollars supporting the criminal justice system, make all of us complicit in that abuse, torture. It takes a mind akin to Hitler's to oversee all the cruelty, especially the solitary confinement in the U.S. criminal justice system. I can't wrap my thoughts around those who claim babies have the right to be born and yet also support and make all those wicked policies and laws that deny the rights of so many young Blacks their freedom and the spirit to pursue happiness. Arrests in the War on Drugs seem to deny that these young Blacks were fetuses too, in the beginning.

According to the *World Book Encyclopedia*, "Back in history people in the ancient and medieval time rarely used imprisonment as a penalty" (Prison, History). Now prison seems to be the first consideration especially for young Blacks. Many developed countries don't have penalties as harsh as the U.S. towards Blacks.

I believe it is because of the many judges like Sherman's that our prisons are filled with unprecedented numbers of Blacks. From my observation, it seems that Hitler wannabes are recruited for judges. Sherman's judge didn't want to try to make our nation a more perfect union. He was indeed the most severe carrier in the pandemic of racism that Sherman encountered.

That judge will be judged by the righteous judge, God, like everybody else.

AFTERWORD

"GOD DIDN'T MAKE NO JUNK," ETHEL WATERS SAID. I AM SOMEBODY cause God didn't make no junk. (Google, "70 Ethel Waters Quotes on joy, positivity, emotions, time etc.") 9/4/2023. Those thousands and thousands of young Black men behind bars, which did include my loved one: are not junk. The Bible says that God made humans in his own image and in Genesis 1:31, that what he made was "very good." Some leaders now want to make their own rules, laws, and policies and changes to discriminate against who and what God made. They concocted the War on Drugs to measure today what and who is good and bad. In all those prisons, they've locked up unprecedented numbers of young Black men, our children, descendants of slaves, and labeled them as bad. However, God said what he made was good. He did not exclude prisoners from sharing in the abundance of the earth. Our leaders have made laws and policies that determine if you're bad because you break the laws made by mostly white men who have faults themselves. Mostly they're trying to punish and silence the voices of young Black men by locking them up. Just as Micah 2:1 says, "it's in the power of their hand." However, if your voice has no power, they wouldn't try to silence it.

Genesis 33:12–13 states that "the children are tender [and need special care along the journey of life] to be able to endure." First Thessalonians 2:7 says "we were gentle…even as a nurse cherisheth her children."

My feelings about my children and grandchildren are passionate. I cherish them. To many Blacks, children are just as tender in their late teens and twenties (when law enforcement policies intensely step up efforts to entrap them (as prisoners) as they did slaves. I'm still just as much older and have had more life experiences than them, along with (ups and downs). They still deserve gentle treatment because I still cherish them as much as ever. They are mine, not villains. I will not ostracize my loved one because evil, racist nay-sayers entrapped him as a prisoner in the evil, racist War on Drugs.

Upon seeing that document *The U.S. vs. Sherman* from a court of law, metaphorically, I likened our U.S government to a vicious roaring lion. In a way, it is like David and Goliath in the Bible. Our children are not just physical beings, but also spiritual "babes in Christ." A babe is defenseless and still needs to depend on someone to do the right thing. The wealth gap and other racial disparities have always affected Blacks. Many are usually in the worst schools and neighborhoods and do not have adequate incomes. Other resources, like bank loans, have also been scarce to unavailable for Blacks' needs to do the right thing for our children.

Ecclesiastes 7:12 says "for wisdom is a defence and money is a defence." However, our past U.S laws and policies, like redlining and others, have intentionally kept Blacks down and behind. Blacks have had to make do, in many cases, with less income and schools often lacking in supplies and not enough caring teachers.

All of this happened with our government's sanction, adding to the Black struggle that's already greater than for any other race. With David and Goliath, David knew about the slingshot and knew how to use one. David's fight was against flesh and blood. With our young Black men today, there's nothing so simple about a young Black man using a sling shot against flesh and blood (Goliath). Instead, a young Black man in the 2000s is compelled to contest the gargantuan

U.S. government with all its mighty tanks, airplanes, expensive surveillance capabilities, and so on—a well-designed unlevel playing field. They stacked the deck to win. I won't stop saying that the government is more like a roaring lion for a poor Black man to defend himself against. However, we encourage ourselves and each other. With God's help, like our ancestors, we have survived since slavery, but many have not.

To repeat, they stacked the deck. Mostly white men made the laws and created the courts. They specifically concocted the War on Drugs where crimes were created and evolved to make more Black felons. It's just another barrier to try and keep as many Blacks as possible at the lowest level of society, as slave owners and municipalities did in colonial America. Why else would they concentrate on the poorer disadvantaged neighborhoods and not on suburban communities to make sweeps to keep Blacks from rising above a certain level as in slavery. You were a slave until your master released you.

To repeat and expound further, "Blacks were disproportionally charged with felonies, in fact, some crimes were specifically defined as felonies" to prevent Blacks from voting (Alexander, 192). Misdemeanors had not usually been punished with that much time behind bars. That's why they concocted the War on Drugs and changed nonviolent drug offenses to felonies to keep the prison population up. According to (Alexander, 2020,144) "thousands of people have had years of their lives wasted in prison—years they would have been free if they had been white".

The U.S system facilitates oppression and accumulates capital from the Black masses through the never-ending discriminatory policies of racism. Unlike COVID in recent years, there's no entity like the CDC to deal with the pandemic of racism.

In the beginning, slave traders went to Africa, a poor continent, and used chains to capture slaves. Today, the police go to the poorer disadvantaged neighborhoods of color and make sweeps. Going to the hood almost guarantees they'll get Blacks.

To repeat, they stacked the deck. I won't stop saying that. The government makes Blacks pay taxes out of what we have left over in the wealth gap. From that, we also have to turn around and help pay the state's lawyer who's against us. Then, for our loved one who is accused, we have to turn around and pay for our own lawyer to defend him or her against breaking what could have been a bad law that the state passed in the first place.

In essence we have to pay the state's lawyer who's against us, and for our own defense lawyer. We have to pay for both of them. Even as the bank uses our deposits, they turn around and deny credit to many of us Blacks for whatever reason. They say there is too little money in an account, but then they take some of that they said was too little and use it for their own inter-office managing purpose. To divert again, only a vicious-minded person likened to a roaring lion would separate a baby from those who love and take care of him or her. Sherman's judge did that. Those who concocted the War on Drugs support policies that do that, just as was done in slavery. Some find pleasure in mistreating others, especially Blacks. That's sadism (finding pleasure in mistreating and harming others), it's a mental illness.

In a metaphoric context, Sherman to me is still a babe in Christ, I repeat, a babe is defenseless but still he's compelled to fight against a roaring lion, as I refer to the U.S. government. Teaching about these injustices and how to defend against them is deliberately left out of the school curriculum to facilitate entrapment. How were young people to know and understand how the criminal justice system operates if it wasn't taught in school? Where were they supposed to learn this from? Ephesians 6:12 expresses what our young Black men and their families have had to face with no studies in prison preparation. The scripture continues, "We wrestle not against flesh and blood, but against principalities [the U.S.

territory] against powers, against the rulers of the darkness of this world, against spiritual wickedness in high places."

Many judges, prosecutors, and others have wicked, biased spirits in these high court positions. They have an evil eye and unequal hand. Anyone who wants to, can see who is locked up.

To reiterate, our young Black men are challenged today to wrestle against the U.S. government with all its might. I still showed gentleness to my loved one, a babe in Christ, having to wrestle with the U.S. government that offensively attacked him and countless other young Blacks. Again, I liken it to a roaring lion who could devour all in its path, including the old and the young, especially Black citizens, the same as it would attack outside invaders of our land. Those in power have stacked the deck like that with an unleveled field, against Blacks especially.

As Alexander states, "It is estimated that three out of four young black men (and nearly all those in the poorest neighborhoods) can expect to serve time in prison". All those young Black men were somebody's baby and have feelings. So do their mothers.

Roe v. Wade was just overturned, meaning that babies have the right to be physically born alive.

Those who overturned *Roe* said nothing about babies also having spirits. It is so unfortunate that so many of those who overturned *Roe v. Wade* mostly advocate banning abortion of the fetus's physical body that they can see with their own eyes. However, God also made the spirit that they can't see with their eyes. The spirit is just as real as the physical. He made both the physical body and the spirit which connect together in life. He made both the physical body and the spirit, interconnected, which together is life. It's so unfortunate too, that many who overturned *Roe v. Wade* have chosen to only show care to save the physical newborn but don't care what happens to that same fetus's spirit in later years. Both the spirit and the physical were connected in the womb.

From my reading, the same scripture that advocates not aborting the fetus came out of the same Bible that also says don't kill the spirit. According to James 2:26, "The body without the spirit is dead." You can't separate the two and still have life as God created it to be. That's why in some catastrophic accidents, where there is so much head injury, medical life support is disconnected. All that thinking, feeling, and mental activity can no longer be the life as God created it.

The message of the masses seems to be don't abort the fetus, the physical newborn. Yet many of the same folks' actions seem to support the idea that it's all right to abort that fetus's spirit. This includes the thinking, feelings, and so on in later years, especially if it's Blacks. God wants us to care for every life at all stages, as he does.

The dictionary defined *spirit* as thinking, etc. In my opinion, many pro-lifers (but not all) don't seem to realize that God cares so much about the spirit too, especially, because in the end, it goes back to God's holy habitation in the sky while the body goes back to the earth. Abortion is further defined as cutting off life or arrested development, and many say that is wrong. Many are against using those chemicals or whatever procedure to abort the fetus which has no voice. However, they support laws that do the same as chemicals: abort and cut off the dreams, aspirations, and feelings especially of young Blacks' spirits in the 2000s. They too mostly have no voice in what is happening to make them four, five, ten, or thirteen to fifty-seven times more likely to be put behind bars than Whites. They had no voice in making laws and policies that most pro-lifers (but not all), see that the fetus needs protection from abortion. However, protection is also needed especially for the spirits of the same young Blacks who were fetuses but grow up. They became targets for entrapment in the criminal justice system as soon as they were big enough, because of the color of their skin. Many pro-lifers can't see that protection of the spirits of the same black fetuses is also needed later, especially when they are teens and young black adults, due to the pandemic of racism.

Instead of using chemicals that arrest development in the womb, many (but not all) don't care about the racist, War on Drugs that attempts (successfully) to crush and abort the feelings, dreams, and aspirations (spirits) of unprecedented numbers of Blacks like my loved one in later years. That massive program, just like slavery, aborts the freedom of many by putting thousands behind bars for months, for years, and maybe for life. This causes separation of many young fathers from their babies and families who need protection. Many of the masses are silent about the laws and policies that make large numbers of blacks so much more likely to be put behind bars for the same drug crimes that are largely ignored when committed by whites. God still cares about what that young Black person and the family is facing because God loves all his children just like many parents love all theirs.

Among the myriad of things used today to abort the spirits, especially of young blacks, the biggest, enabling authority, empowered by our government, is the racist, corrupt criminal justice system and the War on Drugs. Mostly, there is no protection from the War on Drugs, just like entrapment in slavery. There was no protection for slaves being captured with chains and weapons of destruction. Now, likewise, I repeat they have stacked the deck using handcuffs, guns, tanks, surveillance helicopters, and other means in the drug war that our leaders concocted to replace slavery. Our law enforcers use as much fuel as they need, and make from four, five, thirteen on up to over fifty-seven more attempts to capture a young Black, rather than young whites.

That massive program, with seemingly limitless funding, kills the spirits, by intentionally interfering with the thoughts, feelings, and mind of that one captured person who began as a fetus. It affects the whole family, just like in slavery. Thousands of fathers lose their freedom, locked-up in warehouses for varying lengths of time, sometimes for life.

Many support and plan how to abort the dreams of Blacks, like Sherman's history teacher did. For no other reason than the color of their skin. It seems that many are recruited who will help carry out the from school to prison pipeline like the history teacher.

All of those things mentioned above can damage the spirit. To repeat, James 2:26 "the body without the spirit is dead". There's still the physical body left, but in many cases there is also a badly damaged spirit. The body and the spirit are connected. So sometimes what is heard in the mind translates into a headache, high blood pressure, or other ailments.

From my studies of the scripture, I repeat that, God cares for his creation from birth throughout all stages of a person's life. God loves all his children, even those unfairly entrapped and those treated as villains, maligned, rejected, and locked up in unprecedented numbers because of the color of their skin.

Reiterating, those in power stacked the deck because they could. Again, Micah 2:1 says they did it because "it was in the power of their hand." They were compelled by their own racist attitudes of resentment towards Blacks and their outrageous greed and self-interest in spreading the pandemic of racism.

Second Thessalonians 2:10 says, "because of the unrighteousness in them that perish…they received not the love of the truth that they might be saved." Nelson Mandela said that the true character of a society is revealed in how it treats its children.

This nation is exceptional because it treats an overwhelming number of its young men of color (especially Black) like junk. In no other country have I read that one in three of their young minorities is under the control of their criminal justice system and have to navigate through such a narrow channel to have freedom.

Barbara Jordan said, "What the people want is very

simple—they want an America as good as its promise." Google, Barbara Jordan, "Barbara Jordan Quotes." 9/4/2023. There was nothing in the promise about thousands and thousands of the young descendants of slaves being four times, ten times, and up to 80 and, up to 90 times in some states more likely to be arrested in general and sent to federal prison on drug charges than whites. I agree with James Baldwin, who told his nephew in a letter published in 1962, the crime of which "I accuse my country and my countrymen for, which neither I nor time, nor history will ever forgive them" (5). "They are destroying hundreds of lives and do not know it and do not want to know it." Baldwin goes on and writes, those men are your brothers—your lost young brothers. If the word, *integration* means anything, this is what it means: that we, with love shall force our brothers to see themselves as they are to cease fleeing from reality and begin to change it. We can make America what American must become.

I've always been a Christian and believe in forgiveness. Based upon William Paul Young's book *The Shack*, I believe God is still calling theologians with a message for these modern times. Young notes that "Forgiveness does not require me to pretend" that what happened to me never happened (227). Absolutely it's all right to be angry about something so terrible

Racism is terrible and has caused incredible pain to many for ages. Anger is the right response to something so wrong. This twenty-first-century theologian convinced me that I can forgive, but I'm not required to pretend that the thing that happened to us never happened. The Bible says we were made in God's image. God got angry.

The War on Drugs seems to have been declared with Blacks in mind. Why else would law enforcement go to the hood and do sweeps? Just like they went to Africa (not Sweden or Australia) to make slaves, they go to the hood and make criminals.

Since it is reality and because young white men know that Black and Brown people are far more likely to be imprisoned, young and old whites don't care. It's known that whites are just as likely to commit drug crimes, but to repeat, their crimes are more likely to be ignored. To repeat, their crimes are more likely to be ignored. They don't get imprisoned in large numbers as routine. It's just not happening to them, and they know this. Usually that's not reality for many of them. Their drug crimes are largely ignored. Alexander reports that "whites even poor whites—are far less likely to be imprisoned for drug offenses" (196).

Some of our leaders seem to still want to discriminate and keep some remnant of the three-fifths of a person that defined the Negro in America's first Constitution.

In closing, my opinion regarding mass incarceration and racial justice is like Michelle Alexander's. She writes, "Waiting for Whites to be fair, history suggests it will be a long wait. It's not that whites are more unjust than others. Rather, their human nature makes them cling tight to one's advantages and rationalize the suffering and exclusion of others" (2020, 320). My opinion is that many of them took Locke's preaching to heart. He said "feel nothing about others misfortune." He was talking about slaves.

Many citizens (especially Blacks) have experienced that the pandemic of racism is real—and can do great harm. Sherman's racist history teacher put a stumbling block in Sherman's path that derailed further studies for a degree after high school. It was a major hurdle, perhaps for him his first one of that complexity. A few years later, Sherman could have been contemplating a college degree with an SAT of 1500 in the eleventh grade. Instead, he was entrapped in the criminal justice system. Then as he wanted to be a good father like his dad was, Sherman was doing time for a non-violent drug conviction, because of the false, evil, racist War on Drugs. He was blocked from being the dad he wanted to be until his release from prison.

We Blacks often have had to change plans because a wrench from the pandemic of racism was thrown into them.

Just think how many young Blacks find their plans sabotaged as Sherman did because of the color of their skin.

As Michelle Alexander reported, "many wonderful, good-hearted white people were generous to others…and even kind [to some Blacks] but don't believe it is yet "the right time for equality" (2010, 2011, 183). Many (but not all) continue with the racist master plan of denials, hindrances, barriers, self greed and indifference, just like in colonial America.

My final consideration is to divert with a question followed with a request. Did you ever hear of Christmas in July? While visiting family a few weeks ago (it is February 2) for Christmas, we were listening to Christmas music. My daughter said, "Mama, do you remember this song?" It was James Brown singing "Santa Claus Go Straight to the Ghetto." It took me way back to the fun dances in high school, that some of you also probably remember, when we'd dance to his unique screams. That song is still just as relevant and appropriate today for my purpose, as when it was first published. Santa, usually a white man in his sleigh, wasn't shown on TV flying around the ghetto that much.

However, that's where unprecedented numbers of Blacks in mass incarceration today came from. They've always been disproportionately represented as criminals in prison. To repeat, as Marable said, "over half of U.S. prisoners at any one given time are Black" (112).

Perhaps it was not very easy for Santa to find his way to the ghetto. Nevertheless, little Black boys in the ghetto loved getting new things and toys too. To the contrary, in the War on Drugs, law enforcement officers easily found the ghetto first in order to fill prison cells. However, Black neighborhoods had been consistently overlooked by other authorities when it came to building new schools, for example. New jails, however, were built with blacks in mind. In the drug war, TV had no problem showing Black neighborhoods where police did sweeps. Those entrapped in the sweeps are our own beloved children, not villains. A lot of them grew up not having their basic needs met. A part of those little boys is still in our Black young men. My request is similar to James Brown's, but my version is to tell Santa Claus to go straight to the prisons. There you'll find overwhelming Black youth (many from the ghetto) who were unfairly targeted ten times, thirteen times, and as many as eighty to ninety times more likely than whites to be pursued, arrested, convicted, and sent to federal prison for drugs because of the color of their skin.

That song, by James Brown, is still so relevant today.

The *World Book Encyclopedia* describes Santa as a mythical old man who brings gifts to children at Christmas. It further notes that today's Santa did indeed develop from a real person. He was extremely kind and often took presents to the needy. He was friendly and brought cheer. The encyclopedia notes that he became a bishop when only a boy. Those attributes of genuine compassion might be greatly appreciated by most young Black men behind bars.

Prisoners deserve to feel the spirit of Christ also. Christ did not exclude young Black prisoners from his abundant blessings or from having dominion over gold and the onyx stone in Havilah and Ethiopia of our African ancestors (Genesis 2:11–12). Black prisoners are God's children too. Christ brought a spirit that's good in December as well as in July and through all seasons for all people.

Isaiah 61 speaks of preaching good tidings and proclaiming the opening of the prisons to them who are bound. Who is more needy and bound at the same time than young Blacks in the criminal justice system? To me, it mimics the true nature of slavery with the loss of freedom. With all those descriptions of compassion cited in the *World Book Encyclopedia*, my request is indeed that Santa Claus go straight to the prisons. I would go as far as describing the criminal justice system with a majority of Blacks, as a senator did in another context: "it's just slavery under another name."

A timely PBS North Carolina News Weekend broadcast recently showed an interview about Blacks with Nathaniel Harnett, a neuroscientist, on February 12, 2023. Mr. Harnett is an assistant professor of psychiatry at Harvard Medical School. He reported new findings that childhood trauma from early childhood stress from racism, poverty, and so on can have lasting psychological effects. He noted that traumas can change the structure of children's developing brains. He stated that black and white people don't have different brains, but the adversities of racism and discrimination disproportionately burden Black children.

Those adversities impact Blacks more. These are burdens of adversity that many whites don't have. My research says prisons are filled with especially Blacks who hold up a disproportionate burden in prison just like in slavery, when many slaves were not paid for their labor. Similarly, prisoners can't accumulate that much wealth in jail. You can visit the jails and prisons and see for yourselves who is behind bars in greater numbers. White judges, prosecutors, and others are the ones still profiting the most off the misery of a preponderance of Blacks who are locked up.

In spite of the disproportionate share of adversities as already mentioned, the criminal justice system targets our young Blacks, which is allowed by our government. They're four, five, ten, thirteen to fifty-seven times and on up—more likely to go to prison on non-violent drug charges, just like in slavery where slaves were chained and not paid for their time and labor.

Just like in slavery, when they went to Africa to get slaves, they go to neighborhoods where there's been a lot of adversity and poverty, where policies legislate and fund the entrapment of those who are most affected by adversities like racism and discrimination.

You might not be able to preach the gospel in all the world, but you can do what's right in your little corner of the world. The dictionary defines *courage* as bravery or guts. I've paraphrased all that as my meaning for courage: it's: that quality of mind, that spirit to challenge, and the courage to do what one thinks is right.

We hear so often that God is love, but not as often that God is just and righteous. I get my beliefs for living and giving from the Bible. I believe 2 Timothy 3:16, that "All scripture is given by inspiration of God, and is profitable for doctrine, for reproof, for correction, for instruction in righteousness.

I also believe that God is just. Isaiah 4: 21 says so…there is no God else besides me, a just God and Savior.

Matthew 5:18, "till heaven and earth pass, one jot or one tittle shall no wise pass from the law, till all is fulfilled. I haven't heard that preached in ages.

James 5:6, ye have condemned and killed the just, and he doth not resist you. "Too many of our young Blacks, as this scripture says have been condemned and imprisoned for minor offenses. And too many have been outright killed by police, though unarmed.

Revelation 15:3, Lord God Almighty; just and true are thou ways.

P.S.   To divert one last time, a most recent news story that came out on September 28, 2023 validates a lot of what I wrote about in my book from firsthand experiences with my loved one, Sherman.

The report was titled, *U.S. Jail Practices are Racist and an Afront to Human Dignity.* The investigation was set up by the U.N. Human Rights council from three U.N. appointed experts. The report is that U.N. human rights have called for major reforms of the U.S. criminal justice system to combat systemic racism.

Some stories said the situation amounts "to contemporary forms of slavery." Stories account being alarmed at the "widespread use of solitary confinement disproportionately applied to inmates of African descent," Emma Farge, U.S. Jail

Practices are Racist and an Afront to Human Dignity U.N. Experts say (washingtonpost.com, April and May visits, 2023).

Other experts heard first-hand…testimonies of pregnant women shackled during labor, who due to chains, lost their babies. Stories involved Black women.

As I see it, it's slavery under another name, namely, The War on Drugs – Mass Incarceration; with unprecedented numbers of descendants of slaves made prisoners. According to (Alexander, 2010, 2012, 9). One in three young African Americans will serve time in prison, if trends continue.

I'm comparing this to the "n" symbol used in math that stands for an indefinite number (no limits). That seems to be the goal of authorities (an indefinite number), with one in three Blacks under the control of the criminal justice system.

"The critical need for comprehensive reform" is pointed out, Farge, (washingtonpost.com). A new commission on operations for people of African descent is called for.

We as a people have to continue to encourage ourselves and each other as our ancestors have done down through the ages.

I am encouraged that some people say there has been some progress. I feel happy when good happens to other people. But as for myself -- because of what I've been through with my loved one and the criminal justice system, I am not happy. With all the other Blacks behind bars, I'm not happy about that especially with the U.N. report.

Looking back in history though, I get a good feeling that Harriet Tubman (1821?–1913) managed a secret way called the Underground Railroad, for helping slaves escape to the northern states and Canada in the days before the Civil War. This gives me hope, along with the work that contemporaries are doing.

And last but not least, I thank God who makes every day new with new possibilities. Psalm 27:14 says, "Be of good courage and he shall strengthen your heart, all ye that hope in the Lord." It's always the right time to hope in the Lord.

ACKNOWLEDGMENTS

I'm especially grateful to Brian Anthony, who was so gracious to start typing my manuscript.

Thank you so very much to Rachael for completing the lion's share of the typing and editing.

Thank you very much to Joe Fryar for jogging my memory about the *Perry Mason* television show in the 1950s.

Thank you to Walter Weathers for some of my earliest typing.

Deep appreciation for Pat's unwavering favor of prayer.

With deep gratitude to Alisa Washington for helping to finish the typing and editing in a cinch; then doubling back to do some last specific essentials.

Thank you to Eileen, Benita and Ivan, my children, and to Aleah for help with the whatevers.

Last but not least, thank you to Gail Starr for valuable contributions.

REFERENCES

Alexander, Michelle. *The New Jim Crow: Mass Incarceration in the Age of Colorblindness.* New York: The New Press, 2020.

Baldwin, James. *The Fire Next Time.* New York: Vintage Books, 1962

Drug Alliance Policy. "End the Drug War and Undo Its Harm" New York, June 24, 2023

Farge, Emma. "U.S. Jail Practices are Racist and an Affront to Human Dignity; U.N. Experts Say," (washingtonpost.com, April and May visits, 2023).

Harnett, Nathaniel. 2023. "PTSD, Racism and Discrimination Disproportionately Affect Black Children." Interview by Laura Barrón-López. PBS NC News Weekend, February 19, 2023.

Harvard Health Publications, "Vitamins and Minerals," 2006, 16.

Holy Bible. (KJV)

Jordan, Barbara. "Barbara Jordan Quotes, Brainy Quotes, "Google, 9/4/2023, http://www.grainy quote.com/quotes/Barbara-Jordan-103992

Kendi, Ibrahim X. *Stamped from the Beginning: The Definitive History of Racist Ideas in America.* New York: Nation Books, 2016.

Mandela, Nelson. "Nelson Mandela on Children," HuffPost, Google, Dec. 5, 2013, https://www.HuffPost.com/entry/Nelson-Mandela-on-children

Marable, Manning. *How Capitalism Underdeveloped Black America: Problems in Race, Political Economy, and Society.* Chicago, IL: Haymarket Books, 1983.

Mendez, Juan. "Solitary Confinement is Torture, "Psychology Today, Google, May 10, 2018, https://www.psychology today.com/us/blog/talking-about-trauma/201/805/solitaryconfinement-is-torture

Pfaff, John. F. *Locked In: The True Causes of mass incarceration and How to Achieve Real Reform.* New York: Basic Books, 2017.

U.S. Congress. House of Representatives, "Decriminalization of Marijuana" April, 2022, 117th Congress, H.R. 3617

Waggoner, Martha. "Lawsuit Challenges States Use of Solitary Confinement, U.S. News, Oct. 16, 2019

Walkenhurst, Emily. WRAL News, Oct., 2023, https://wral//IQYMF

Warnock, Senator. Rev. Raphael, "Warnock for Georgia Campaign Ad, Washington D.C.

Waters, Ethel. "70 Ethel Waters Quotes on Joy, Positivity, emotions,Time, ETC" Google, 9/4/2023, https://quotesthe famouspeople.com/ethel-waters-1374.phb

World Book Encyclopedia. Field Enterprises Educational Corporation, Chicago, 1973

Young, William Paul. *The Shack.* Newbury Park, CA: Windblown Media, 2007.